What is Born of the Spirit is Spirit

What is Born of the Spirit is Spirit

A Biblical Spirituality of Spirit

Mark G. Boyer

WIPF & STOCK · Eugene, Oregon

WHAT IS BORN OF THE SPIRIT IS SPIRIT
A Biblical Spirituality of Spirit

Copyright © 2019 Mark G. Boyer. All rights reserved. Except for brief quotations in critical publications or reviews, no part of this book may be reproduced in any manner without prior written permission from the publisher. Write: Permissions, Wipf and Stock Publishers, 199 W. 8th Ave., Suite 3, Eugene, OR 97401.

Wipf & Stock
An Imprint of Wipf and Stock Publishers
199 W. 8th Ave., Suite 3
Eugene, OR 97401

www.wipfandstock.com

PAPERBACK ISBN: 978-1-5326-9713-5
HARDCOVER ISBN: 978-1-5326-9714-2
EBOOK ISBN: 978-1-5326-9715-9

Manufactured in the U.S.A.   09/30/19

The Scripture quotations contained herein are from the New Revised Standard Version Bible, copyright © 1989 by the Division of Christian Education of the National Council of the Churches of Christ in the U.S.A., and are used by permission. All rights reserved.

Dedicated to the Past and Present Owners
of DeSales Catholic Bookstore,
Springfield, Missouri:
Larry Sloan
Larry and Sue Frey
Tracy L. King

"... [W]hat is born of the Spirit is spirit."

—John 3:6

"... [I]t is that very Spirit bearing witness with our spirit that we are children of God...."

—Romans 8:16

"... [T]hese things God has revealed to us through the Spirit; for the Spirit searches everything, even the depths of God. For what human being knows what is truly human except the human spirit that is within? So also no one comprehends what is truly God's except the Spirit of God. Now we have received not the spirit of the world, but the Spirit that is from God, so that we may understand the gifts bestowed on us by God. And we speak of these things in words not taught by human wisdom but taught by the Spirit, interpreting spiritual things to those who are spiritual."

—1 Corinthians 2:10–13

"... [A]nyone united to the Lord becomes one spirit with him."

—1 Corinthians 6:17

"Now the Lord is the Spirit, and where the Spirit of the Lord is, there is freedom. And all of us, with unveiled faces, seeing the glory of the Lord as though reflected in a mirror, are being transformed into the same image from one degree of glory to another; for this comes from the Lord, the Spirit."

—2 Corinthians 3:17–18

Contents

Abbreviations | ix
Notes on the Bible | xiii
Notes on The Roman Missal | xvii
Introduction | xxi
    A Short Biblical Pneumatology, This Book

1 **God and Spirit** | 1
    Spirit in Spirit 1, Sent from on High, Spirit is Life, Spirit Gives Life, Spirit-Breath, Spirit of the LORD, Paraclete, Spirit Seeks Spirit 1, Spirit in Spirit 2, Through Spirit, The Lord be with Your Spirit, Spirit Returned, Spirit Seeks Spirit 2

2 **Spirit as Gift** | 16
    Gift of Spirit, Gifts of the Spirit, Spirit Poured Out 1, Spirit Poured Out 2, Spirit Put Upon 1, Spirit Put Upon 2, Filled with Spirit 1, Filled with Spirit 2, Fire of Spirit, Spirit Rests On, Bestowed Spirit, Grace of the Spirit, Gentle-Kindly-Patient Spirit, Good-Quiet-Noble Spirit, Dauntless Spirit, Fruits of Spirit

3 **Spirit Speaks** | 37
    Spirit of Father Speaks, Spirit Reveals, Spirit Testifies, Spirit Captive, Spirit Comes Upon, Spirit Takes Possession, Spirit Stirred 1, Spirit Stirred 2, Spirit Guide

4 **Powerful Spirit** | 48
    Power of the Spirit 1, Power of the Spirit 2, Laying on of Hands, Spirit Fire, Spirit Breath, Spirit and Power, Anointing Spirit, Spiritual Seal, Adoptive Spirit, Temple of Spirit, Work of the Spirit, Drink the Spirit, Without Spirit

5 **Spiritual Results** | 66
Promised Spirit, Spiritual Perception, Spiritual Endowment, Spiritual Sharing, Spiritual Accompaniment, Spiritual Sanctification, Spiritual Unity, Willing Spirit, Prayer in the Spirit, Spiritual Blessing

6 **Water and Spirit** | 79
Baptism in the Spirit, Water and Dove, Born of Water and Spirit, Water and Wind, New Spirit, Refreshed Spirit, Spiritual Transformation, Different Spirit

7 **Led by the Spirit** | 90
Guided by Spirit, David Led by Spirit, Mary Led by Spirit, Jesus Led by Spirit, Spirit Teacher, Spirit of Wisdom, Spirit of Understanding, Spirit of Counsel, Spirit of Fortitude, Spirit of Knowledge, Spirit of Piety, Spirit of Fear of the Lord

8 **Miscellaneous Spirit** | 107
Worship in Spirit, Spirit of Love, Joy in Spirit, Spirit of Justice, Humble in Spirit, Broken Spirit, Grieved in Spirit, Disciplined Spirit

9 **Evil Spirit** | 117
Blasphemy against the Spirit, Evil Spirit, Unclean Spirit, Seized by a Spirit, Fainting Spirit, Troubled Spirit, Proud Spirit, Bitter Spirit, Crushed in Spirit, Downcast in Spirit, Lying Spirit, Hardened Spirit, Spirit of Confusion, Testing the Spirit, Spirit of Divination, Gliding Spirit

Bibliography | 139
Recent Books by Mark G. Boyer published by Wipf & Stock | 143

Abbreviations

BCE = Before the Common Era (same as BC = Before Christ)

CB (NT) = Christian Bible (New Testament)

Acts = Acts of the Apostles
Col = Letter to the Colossians
1 Cor = First Letter of Paul to the Corinthians
2 Cor = Second Letter of Paul to the Corinthians
Eph = Letter to the Ephesians
Gal = Letter of Paul to the Galatians
Heb = Letter to the Hebrews
Jas = Letter of James
John = John's Gospel
1 John = First Letter of John
Jude = Letter of Jude
Luke = Luke's Gospel
Mark = Mark's Gospel
Matt = Matthew's Gospel
1 Pet = First Letter of Peter
2 Pet = Second Letter of Peter
Phil = Letter of Paul to the Philippians
Phlm = Letter of Paul to Philemon
Rev = Revelation
Rom = Letter of Paul to the Romans
1 Thess = First Letter of Paul to the Thessalonians
2 Thess = Second Letter to the Thessalonians
1 Tim = First Letter to Timothy
2 Tim = Second Letter to Timothy

Titus = Letter to Titus

CCC = *Catechism of the Catholic Church*
CE = Common Era (same as AD = *Anno Domini*, in the year of the Lord)
cf. = confer, compare

HB (OT) = Hebrew Bible (Old Testament)

1 Chr = First Book of Chronicles
2 Chr = Second Book of Chronicles
Dan = Daniel
Deut = Deuteronomy
Eccl = Ecclesiastes
Exod = Exodus
Ezek = Ezekiel
Ezra = Ezra
Gen = Genesis
Hab = Habakkuk
Hag = Haggai
Hos = Hosea
Isa = Isaiah
Jer = Jeremiah
Job = Job
Joel = Joel
Josh = Joshua
Judg = Judges
1 Kgs = First Book of Kings
2 Kgs = Second Book of Kings
Mal = Malachi
Mic = Micah
Neh = Nehemiah
Num = Numbers
Prov = Proverbs
Ps(s) = Psalm(s)
1 Sam = First Book of Samuel
2 Sam = Second Book of Samuel
Zech = Zechariah

NABRE = New American Bible Revised Edition
NRSV = New Revised Standard Version

OC = Order of Confirmation

OT (A) = Old Testament (Apocrypha)

    Add Esth = Additions to Esther
    Bar = Baruch
    2 Esd = Second Book of Esdras
    Jdt = Judith
    1 Macc = First Book of Maccabees
    2 Macc = Second Book of Maccabees
    4 Macc = Fourth Book of Maccabees
    Sg Three = Song of the Three Jews (Prayer of Azariah)
    Sir = Sirach (Ecclesiasticus)
    Tob = Tobit
    Wis = Wisdom (of Solomon)

par. = paragraph
pars. = paragraphs
RM = *The Roman Missal*

Notes on the Bible

THE BIBLE IS DIVIDED into two parts: The Hebrew Bible (Old Testament) and the Christian Bible (New Testament). The Hebrew Bible consists of thirty-nine named books, written roughly between 1200 and 164 BCE, accepted by Jews and Protestants as Holy Scripture. The Old Testament also contains those thirty-nine books plus seven to fifteen more named books or parts of books called the Apocrypha or the Deuterocanonical Books; the Old Testament is accepted by Catholics and several other Christian denominations as Holy Scripture. The Christian Bible, consisting of twenty-seven named books, written between 50 and 115 CE, is also called the New Testament; it is accepted by Christians as Holy Scripture. Thus, in this work:

—Hebrew Bible (Old Testament), abbreviated HB (OT), indicates that a book is found both in the Hebrew Bible and the Old Testament;

—Old Testament (Apocrypha), abbreviated OT (A), indicates that a book is found only in the Old Testament Apocrypha and not in the Hebrew Bible;

—and Christian Bible (New Testament), abbreviated CB (NT), indicates that a book is found only in the Christian Bible or New Testament.

In notating biblical texts, the first number refers to the chapter in the book, and the second number refers to the verse within the chapter. Thus, HB (OT) Isa 7:11 means that the quotation comes from Isaiah, chapter 7, verse 11. OT (A) Sirach 39:30 means that the quotation comes from Sirach, chapter 39, verse 30. CB (NT) Mark 6:2 means that the quotation comes from Mark's Gospel, chapter 6, verse 2. When more than one sentence appears in a verse, the letters a, b, c, etc. indicate the sentence being referenced in the verse. Thus, HB (OT) 2 Kgs 1:6a means that the quotation comes from the Second Book of Kings, chapter 1, verse 6, sentence 1. Also, poetry, such as the Psalms and sections of Judith, Proverbs, and Isaiah, may be noted using the letters a, b, c, etc. to indicate the lines being used. Thus, Psalm 16:4a refers to the first line of verse 4 of Psalm 16; there are two more lines of verse 4: b and c.

In the HB (OT) and the OT (A), the reader often sees LORD (note all capital letters). Because God's name (Yahweh or YHWH, referred to as the Tetragrammaton) is not to be pronounced, the name Adonai (meaning *Lord*) is substituted for Yahweh when a biblical text is read. When a biblical text is translated and printed, LORD (cf. Gen 2:4) is used to alert the reader to what the text actually states: Yahweh. Furthermore, when the biblical author writes Lord Yahweh, printers present Lord GOD (note all capital letters for GOD; cf. Gen 15:2) to avoid the printed ambiguity of LORD LORD. When the reference is to Jesus, the word printed is Lord (note capital L and lower case letters; cf. Luke 11:1). When writing about a lord (note all lower case letters (cf. Matt 18:25) with servants, no capital L is used.

Presuppositions

The HB (OT) begins as stories passed on by word of mouth from one person to another. Sometime during the oral transmission stage, authors decide to collect the oral stories and write them. Because oral stories can be told in many different ways, biblical authors often retain what we have come to learn is the same basic story told in two different ways. A good example of this is the account of Noah, which represents the merger of two different stories into one in its present form. A change occurs immediately when oral stories are written. One does not tell a story the same way one writes a story. Repetition and correction occur in oral story-telling. Except for future emendations by copyists, single statements by characters and plot structure guides dominate written stories. Furthermore, in both oral and written story-telling, types or models are employed. In the CB (NT) Elizabeth becomes a type of Hannah, who is herself a type of Sarah. When orally narrating or writing a story, the teller or author consciously creates one character as a type of another in order to make the character and his or her words and actions intelligible to the hearer or reader.

In the CB (NT) the oldest gospel is Mark's account of Jesus' victory. The author of Matthew's Gospel copied and shortened about eighty percent of Mark's material into his book and then added other stories to make the work longer. The author of Luke's Gospel copied and shortened about fifty percent of Mark's material into his orderly account and then added other stories to make the work much longer. Then, the author of Luke's Gospel wrote a second volume—The Acts of the Apostles—which compliments his first volume. Mark's Gospel begins as oral story-telling, lasting for about forty years in that form. An unidentified author, called Mark for the sake of convenience, collects the oral stories, sets a plot, and writes the first gospel around 70 CE. Because Jesus was expected to return soon, no one had thought about recording what he had said and done until Mark came along and realized that he was not returning as quickly as had been thought. About ten years after Mark finished his gospel, Matthew needed to adopt Mark's narrative—originally intended for a peasant Gentile readership—to a Jewish audience. And about twenty years after Mark finished his gospel, Luke needed to adapt Mark's poor Gentile-intended work for a rich, upper class, urban, Gentile readership. The author of Luke's Gospel also needed to present the activity of the leaders of the church while all waited the not-so-imminent return of Jesus. The author of John's Gospel did not know the existence of the other three works collectively named synoptic gospels.

In addition to the material the authors of Matthew's Gospel and Luke's Gospel copied from Mark's Gospel, both the author of Matthew's Gospel and the author of Luke's Gospel had another common source; this source is named Q by biblical scholars. Q is the abbreviation for *Quelle*, a German word meaning *source*. In general, the source seems to be sayings of Jesus which each author placed into narratives deemed appropriate. Thus, when a saying like Matthew 5:3 and Luke 6:20 are almost identical in wording, biblical scholars consider the source of the saying to be Q. Or the short parable known as the leaven, found in Matthew 13:33 and Luke 13:20–21, is Q material.

Furthermore, gospels were not first intended to be read privately as is done today. They were meant to be heard in a group. The very low rate of literacy in the first century would have never dictated many copies of texts since most people could not read, and their standard practice was to listen to another read the stories to them. Thus, what began as oral story-telling passed on by word of mouth became written story-telling preserved in gospels. A careful reading of Mark's Gospel will reveal the orality still embedded in the text, especially evident in the repetition of words and the organization of stories in three parts. In rewriting Mark, Matthew and Luke remove the last traces of oral story-telling.

There are genuine Pauline letters, and biblical scholars have identified second-generation Pauline letters. Genuine Pauline letters are those written by or dictated by Paul, such as Romans, First and Second Corinthians, and Galatians. Second-generation Pauline letters are those written by someone else after Paul was dead in order to deal with issues in the early church communities that Paul could not have foreseen; second-generation Pauline letters, such as Colossians, Ephesians, and Second Thessalonians, are written in the name of Paul by an anonymous author in order to give them Pauline authority.

Notes on *The Roman Missal*

The Roman Missal

THE ROMAN MISSAL IS the book of prayers used by a priest or bishop when celebrating the Eucharist, commonly referred to as saying Mass. In 1970, following the close of the Second Vatican Council, Pope Paul VI issued a new Roman Missal in Latin replacing the one issued by Pope Pius V in 1570 after the close of the Council of Trent. The Missal of Paul VI was emended in 1971 and issued in English in 1974. In 1975, a second edition in Latin was issued by Paul VI; it was issued in English in 1985. A third edition of *The Roman Missal* was issued in Latin by Pope John Paul II in 2002 and emended in 2008; however, it was not until 2011 that *The Roman Missal* was issued in English. Thus, all references made to *The Roman Missal*, abbreviated RM, in this book refer to the 2011 English edition.

Here are some terms used in *The Roman Missal* with which the reader may not be familiar:

Advent Season = The Advent Season begins four Sundays before Christmas, December 25. It begins on the last Sunday of November or the First Sunday of December. It ends at 4 p.m. on December 24. It has two foci: the return of Christ in glory and preparation to celebrate his birth in Bethlehem.

Christmas Season = The Christmas Season begins at 4 p.m. on December 24 and lasts until the second Sunday of January, the Feast of the Baptism of the Lord. It lasts about three weeks.

Celebration of the Eucharist = The Celebration of the Eucharist, commonly referred to as the Mass, consists of two parts: the Liturgy of the Word (two or three Scripture texts, a homily, the Creed, and General

Intercessions) and the Liturgy of the Eucharist (a Eucharistic Prayer, the Our Father, and communion).

Collect = This is the opening prayer of the Eucharist (Mass) introduced by the priest or bishop with "Let us pray." It collects all the prayers of the congregants into one general, all-inclusive prayer.

Communion Antiphon = The Communion Antiphon is a verse from Scripture that is sung or recited at the beginning of Communion.

Easter Season = The Easter Season begins on Easter Sunday of the Resurrection of the Lord and lasts for fifty days. It ends with Pentecost Sunday. Easter Sunday is the first Sunday after the first full moon after the Spring or Vernal Equinox.

Entrance Antiphon = The Entrance Antiphon is a verse from Scripture that is sung or recited at the beginning of Mass.

Eucharistic Prayer = This is the most important prayer of the Mass prayed by a priest or a bishop. During the narrative of all thirteen choices, the priest or bishop takes bread and remembers what Jesus did before he died—giving his body as bread—and takes a cup of wine and remembers what Jesus did before he died—giving his blood as wine. The prayer also includes a petition to God to send the Holy Spirit to make the bread and wine the body and blood of Christ as well as petitions for the pope, the local bishop, all the faithful, and the dead. It ends with a doxology to which all respond "Amen."

Lenten Season = The Season of Lent begins with Ash Wednesday, seven weeks before Easter. Lent ends on Holy Thursday evening, the Thursday before Easter Sunday.

Liturgical Year = The liturgical year begins with the First Sunday of Advent, usually the last Sunday of November or the first Sunday of December; The Advent Season lasts for four weeks. The Christmas Season begins on December 25, lasts three weeks, and ends with the Feast of the Baptism of the Lord, usually the second Sunday of January. The Lenten Season begins with Ash Wednesday, which can occur anytime in February or early March; it lasts six weeks and ends at the beginning of The Sacred Paschal Triduum with Thursday of the Lord's Supper, which can occur anytime from late March into early April. The Sacred Paschal Triduum ends on Easter Sunday evening. The Easter Season begins with Easter Sunday of the Resurrection of the Lord—usually falling in late March or early April—lasts fifty days, and ends with Pentecost Sunday, falling anytime between the middle of May and early June. In between the Christmas Season and the Lenten Season and in between the Easter

Season and the next Advent is the Season of Ordinary Time—meaning counted weeks. The first section of Ordinary Time can be from two to ten weeks, and the second section of Ordinary Time can be from eleven to thirty-four weeks.

Mass = In *The Roman Missal*, Mass refers to the two parts of the Celebration of the Eucharist: the Liturgy of the Word and the Liturgy of the Eucharist. The word *Mass*, from the Latin *missa*—from the Latin *mittere*, meaning *to send*—means to send away. The last line of the Mass in Latin is "Ite, missa est.," meaning "Go, the Mass is ended."

Prayer after Communion = This is a concluding prayer said by the priest or bishop after communion—the sharing of the body and blood of Christ—has finished.

Prayer over the Offerings = This is a prayer said by the priest or bishop after the gifts of bread and wine have been prepared, presented to God, and set on the altar.

Prayer over the People = This is a required prayer during Lent which follows the Prayer after Communion. While it may be used at other times, during Lent it asks God to bless people with his divine presence and help them during their journey through Lent to Easter.

Preface = This prayer, introduced with dialogue between the priest or bishop and the congregants, praises and thanks God for something specific, such as the resurrection of Christ. It begins the Eucharistic Prayer and concludes with the Holy, Holy, Holy Lord acclamation. When several choices are provided, they are numbered, such as, Preface I of Easter, Preface II of Easter, etc.

All prayers of any kind in *The Roman Missal* are specified for every day of the liturgical year. Thus, in this book one may find a reference to Monday of the Third Week of Lent; this means that a set of prayers for the Eucharist on Monday of the Third Week of Lent is provided. A set consists of an Entrance Antiphon, a Collect, a Prayer over the Offerings, a Communion Antiphon, a Prayer after Communion, and, during Lent, a Prayer over the People. Likewise, Thursday of the Fifth Week of Easter presents an Entrance Antiphon, a Collect, a Prayer over the Offerings, a Communion Antiphon, and a Prayer after Communion. The prayers are addressed to God through Christ in the unity of the Holy Spirit.

Because *The Roman Missal* is a book of over 1,500 pages, it is subdivided by liturgical seasons (Advent, Christmas, Lent, Easter, and Ordinary Time), feasts, saints, ritual Masses, and more. Some subsections of *The Roman Missal* contain numbered paragraphs. Thus, when a reference appears in a footnote, it will often contain *par.*, the abbreviation for the word *paragraph*, or *pars.*, the abbreviation for the word *paragraphs*, when a range of numbered paragraphs are being referenced within a named subsection of *The Roman Missal*. Other subsections of *The Roman Missal* are not numbered. When this is the case, a page number is given in the footnote to the edition of *The Roman Missal* found in the bibliography of this book; this later case is indicated by only the page number.

The subsections of the RM are indicated in the footnotes and can be found in the Bibliography. In this book, page numbers refer to the edition of the RM in the Bibliography. While page numbers will differ in other published editions of the RM, the detailed information provided in the footnotes is designed to pinpoint where the references can be found in any edition of the RM.

Introduction

A Short Biblical Pneumatology[1]

Words for Spirit

THE HEBREW WORD FOR breath, air, wind, or spirit is *ruach*. It appears about four hundred times in the HB (OT) and the OT (A). Depending on the English translation, *ruach*'s first appearance in the Bible can be at Genesis 1:2. *The New Revised Standard Version* (NRSV) states that a wind from God swept over the face of the waters, but has a footnote indicating that the phrase could also be translated as the spirit of God swept over the waters. *The Contemporary English Version* (CEV) states that the Spirit of God was moving over the water. Just as we are getting started, it is important to note that the NRSV does not capitalize the s of spirit, but the CEV does! The immediate implication for the reader is the reference to spirit, usually understood to be the human spirit, and the reference to Spirit, usually understood to be the divine Spirit. However, in Hebrew there are no capital letters! Thus, when translators from Hebrew to English capitalize or do not capitalize the s of spirit, they are interpreting the meaning of an otherwise ambiguous text. Furthermore, translators have settled on only one meaning of the word *ruach*, which is used for breath, air, wind,

---

1. Pneumatology, from the Greek word *pneuma*, meaning breath, air, wind, or spirit, is the theology of the Holy Spirit, but it is also the study of spirits and spiritual beings.

and spirit—both human and divine! As we will see in the chapters of this book, there are many ways to plumb the plural meanings of *ruach* in the HB (OT) and the OT (A).

The ambiguity associated with *ruach* does not disappear in the CB (NT). The Greek word for breath, air, wind, or spirit is *pneuma*. It appears nearly four hundred times. Just as in Hebrew there are no capital letters, so in ancient Greek there were no capital letters. Thus, not only is the translation of the word as breath, air, wind, or spirit an interpretation of the text in which it appears, but when it is translated, putting a capital S or a lowercase s on it is a further interpretation of the text. For example, in the CB (NT), the first appearance of *pneuma* in the NRSV is Matthew 1:18b: "When [Jesus'] mother Mary has been engaged to Joseph, but before they lived together, she was found to be with child from the Holy Spirit." The phrase—"from the Holy Spirit"—could just as well be translated "from the holy breath," "from the holy air," or "from the holy wind." The noncapitalized phrase in Greek is a descriptive title—not a name—for God's manifestation as a spirit being or a Spirit Being. Likewise, in Mark 2:8, Jesus perceives in his spirit (*pneuma*)—where the translators chose no capital S—but in Mark 1:10, the Spirit descends upon Jesus—where the translators chose a capital S.

In general in the NRSV, which is used throughout this book, translators of the HB (OT) and OT (A) do not use a capital S for *ruach* in any of its phrases, such as the spirit of the LORD. In the CB (NT), however, translators do use a capital S for *pneuma* especially when the word *holy* describes it. In this book, the Scripture that begins each reflection follows the NRSV use; if NRSV does not capitalize s for spirit, neither do I; if NRSV does capitalize S for Spirit or Holy Spirit, so do I. However, in the Reflection that follows the Scripture, I use Spirit to refer to the divine Spirit and spirit to refer to the human spirit. Because there is no way to tell how the writer of the text intended to use either *ruach* or *pneuma*—breath, air, wind, or spirit—I have chosen to let the ambiguity remain in order to plumb the richness of the spiritual benefits that exist in the biblical text. In other words, just as translators decide which meaning of the words to use in English, I have decided to let the words mean all that they can mean in this work.

Spirit (spirit) exists in the HB (OT) and in the OT (A) before it appears in the CB (NT). However, the doctrine of the Trinity—one God, three coequal persons of Father, Son, and Holy Spirit—does not exist in the HB (OT), the OT (A), or the CB (NT). The doctrine of the Holy Spirit begins with the Ecumenical Council of Nicaea I in 325 CE and continues to develop until the end of the Ecumenical Council of Constantinople I in 381 CE. The issue known as *filioque*—referring to the Holy Spirit proceeding from the Father and the Son—was not settled until the Council of Florence in 1439 CE. Before doctrine, there was Scripture. Thus, in this book we are exploring *ruach*—with all its meanings—in the HB (OT) and OT (A)—and *pneuma*—with all its meanings—in the CB (NT).

Metaphorical Language

A metaphor applies a word or phrase to somebody or something that is not meant literally but to make a comparison. An example can be found in the HB (OT) book of Exodus. The LORD tells Moses that he has filled a certain man with divine Spirit (Exod 31:3). In the way that one fills a canteen with water, God fills a man with Spirit. A simile is a figure of speech that draws a comparison between two different things, especially a phrase containing the word *like* or *as*. In the CB (NT), the author of the Acts of the Apostles describes the filling of Jesus' followers with the Holy Spirit, stating, "Divided tongues, as of fire, appeared among them, and a tongue rested on each of them" (Acts 2:3). Thus, being filled with the Spirit is like having a tongue of fire resting on a person, turning him or her into a bush that is blazing but not consumed (Exod 3:2).

Spirit cannot be captured in words; it cannot be possessed, boxed, or defined. It is without form. That is both the beauty of ambiguity—breath, air, wind, and spirit—and the challenge of writing about the biblical Spirit and spirit. ". . . [I]n Christian tradition, the Holy Spirit has 'largely remained the unknown God' since Scripture never really describes the third person of the Trinity."[2] Yet, Scripture presents multiple metaphors

2. Walsh, *Chasing Mystery*, 35.

and similes—such as breath, air, wind, fire, dove, and water—and "[s]omehow the Holy Spirit animates the text, flowing through the spaces of its densely knitted fabric as *textus*, just as it animates the human being."[3] Rohr says, "Ordinary matter is the hiding place for Spirit."[4] ". . . Since the very beginning of time, God's Spirit has been revealing its glory and goodness through the physical creation."[5] Because spirit—along with breath, air, and wind—is invisible, in order to begin to comprehend Spirit and spirit, we need something visible in creation. And the ambiguous meanings of *ruach* and *pneuma* begin to serve our needs while reminding us that the invisible Spirit and spirit are manifest or made visible through matter, but they are not matter. According to Rohr, "All matter reveals Spirit, and Spirit needs matter to 'show itself'!"[6] Thus, "the supernatural and natural world constantly intersect."[7] Matter—breath, air, wind, fire, and dove—reveals Spirit to spirit—and is the means for spirit to encounter Spirit. Then, "[t]he holy vanishes just as quickly as it manifested."[8] According to Walsh, "Humankind [spirit] cannot withstand continued divine presence [Spirit], for it would arrest its faith and life."[9] When all is said, the most we can say about Spirit is this: (nothing, silence).[10] And when we have said (nothing, silence), we have said all!

This book is an exercise in spiritual, biblical metaphor-and-simile reclamation. It is an attempt to recover the spirituality of biblical stories that narrate how the Spirit connects to spirit and the results of such connectivity. By exploring the use of biblical metaphors and similes we develop a spirituality of Spirit, a way of the human spirit being in the presence of the divine Spirit and living accordingly.

A new metaphor for Spirit is electricity, which invisibly runs throughout a house or office. It presents multiple access points—called plugs—which are visible signs of invisible power. It runs or gives life to refrigerators, air conditioners, computers, coffee makers, microwave ovens, etc. Without it, we cannot cool food or ourselves, surf the internet,

3. Ibid., 42.
4. Rohr, *Universal Christ*, 8.
5. Ibid., "Coherence."
6. Ibid., "From the Beginning."
7. Walsh, *Chasing Mystery*, 77.
8. Ibid., 78.
9. Ibid., 138.
10. Boyer, *Shhh! The Sound of Sheer Silence*.

make coffee, or cook; electricity is life-giving. Whether we are aware of it or not, we are surrounded by it and, while not literally true, we are metaphorically plugged into it. Thus, the Spirit is like electricity.

Spirit is also like water: a lake, a river, an ocean.[11] Our spirits are like fish immersed in water. In the underwater world of insightful depth, everything there lives in water. The fish's gills, the coral, the plants, etc. (spirit) take oxygen out of the water (Spirit) for life. Thus, the Spirit is like water.

We can state that the Spirit is like sound coming from the huge speakers displayed on the stage for a concert. Sound fills the entire venue with sound waves that bounce off walls, tables, and people. The eardrums of spirits are attuned to the waves of Spirit-sound, and they hear the sound and are transformed by it (the music). Furthermore, all spirits are connected by the sound of the music to which they are listening. Thus, Spirit is like sound.

Spirit is like gravity; it affects not only spirits, but time and space as well. We spirits are grounded, rooted in it. Because space, the universe, is always expanding, always in motion, all human embodied spirits on earth are engulfed in the gravity and space of the universe. Thus, Spirit is like gravity, Spirit is like space, about which we are usually unaware!

Spirituality Thesis

Spirituality is Spirit connecting to spirit. It is Spirit giving birth to spirit; according to John's Gospel, ". . . [W]hat is born of the Spirit is spirit" (John 3:6). It is Spirit breathing life into spirit; "[s]urely everyone stands as a mere breath," sings the psalmist (Ps 39:5b). Walsh writes, "Biblically, breath signifies both the breath in a living being and the larger element

---

11. I am indebted to Corbin S. Cole for the following similes for Spirit and spirit.

of wind."¹² Spirituality is Spirit blowing windy air into spirit. "The wind cannot be seen," states Sheed; "the wind is powerful; it is the least material of material things, the least earthy of the things that affect earth; its home is the sky."¹³ Because "God is spirit, . . . those who worship him must worship in spirit and truth," states the Johannine Jesus (John 4:24). According to the HB (OT) book of Proverbs, "The human spirit is the lamp of the LORD, searching every inmost part" (Prov 20:27).

Spirit seeks to connect to spirit in order to become tangible, available to the senses, since it has no form. What Walsh writes about holy sites is also true of the Spirit. "A cultic site, a temple, a bush, a tomb, a relic does not contain the holy. Instead, holiness is experienced in the encounter itself; the relationship that it heralds remains vital long after the site of its occurrence does."¹⁴ In other words, breath, air, and wind do not contain the Spirit, but spirit encounters Spirit through the experience of breath, air, and wind; the awareness that the experience heralds remains vital long after the encounter is over. Mutual desiring and divine indwelling is the intended impact of Spirit connecting to spirit.

In his First Letter to the Corinthians, Paul explains: ". . . [A]nyone united to the Lord [Jesus Christ] becomes one spirit with him" (1 Cor 6:17). In his Second Letter to the Corinthians, he adds, ". . . [A]ll of us . . . seeing the glory of the Lord as though reflected in a mirror, are being transformed into the same image from one degree of glory to another; for this comes from the Lord, the Spirit" (2 Cor 3:18). Those who believe that Jesus died and God raised Christ from the dead are united to Christ Jesus, forming one body and becoming one Spirit with him. As a member of the body of Christ, we see the glory of the Spirit reflected in breath, air, wind, water, and fire, and our spirits are transformed into the same image from one degree to glory to another by the Spirit. The result is "the communion of the Holy Spirit" (2 Cor 13:13).

Spirit in the Bible is an invisible force; it is like wind, felt but not seen. Paul presents this idea in his First Letter to the Corinthians, writing that God reveals himself "to us through the Spirit; for the Spirit searches everything, even the depths of God. For what human being knows what is truly human except the human spirit that is within? So also no one comprehends what is truly God's except the Spirit of God" (1 Cor 2:10–11).

---

12. Walsh, *Chasing Mystery*, 95.
13. Sheed, *Knowing God*, 60.
14. Walsh, *Chasing Mystery*, 79.

Thus, according to Paul, we have received "the Spirit that is from God, so that we may understand the gifts bestowed on us by God. And we speak . . . in words not taught by human wisdom but taught by the Spirit, interpreting spiritual things to those who are spiritual" (1 Cor 2:12–13). In his Second Letter to the Corinthians, the apostle adds, "Now the Lord is the Spirit, and where the Spirit of the Lord is, there is freedom" (2 Cor 3:17). The author of the Letter to the Ephesians understood his Pauline source, writing that through Christ Jesus, we now "have access in one Spirit to the Father" (Eph 2:18). We have access to God because the Spirit connects to our spirits and establishes a pipeline through which divine life flows.

Spirit is another way to speak and write about divine presence, which is particularly signified by the elements of theophanies, twenty-one tangible elements signifying God's presence without the elements being God. Among those twenty-one elements are the following which also serve as tangible signs of the Spirit's presence: fire, water, and wind.[15] "The Spirit of God [is] simply God himself . . . ," writes Sheed.[16] Spirit is the word for the divine presence breathed into people, hovering over people, flaming before people, giving life to people. It is like fire, water, wind, or a dove, but it is not any one of those. In the CB (NT) divine presence became incarnate in Jesus of Nazareth, who was named Emmanuel, which means God is with us (Matt 1:23). The divine energy or divine power of the Spirit seeks to connect to the human spirit; this act of connecting is spirituality. According to Rohr, "God must reveal God's self *in you* before God can fully reveal God's self *to you*."[17] We can rephrase this truth in light of our topic: The Spirit must reveal the Spirit's self *in you* before the Spirit can fully reveal Spirit's self *to your spirit*.

Sheed says, "The spirit radiates energies by which the body lives and functions."[18] Living the connection of Spirit to spirit is spirituality. "Alone of the spirits known to us," states Sheed, "the human spirit is a soul—that is to say the life principle of a body—just as we know of no soul but [human's] which is a spirit."[19] Therefore, by referencing the quote above from John's Gospel (4:24), Sheed states, "The God we worship is spirit; our

---

15. Boyer, *Divine Presence*, 42–48, 64–73, 107–112.
16. Sheed, *Knowing God*, 258.
17. Rohr, "An Interior Faith."
18. Sheed, *Knowing God*, 66.
19. Ibid.,

own spirit (which is spirit embodied) is what we worship with."[20] This, of course, is nothing other than Spirit connected to spirit.

Spirit becomes more and more incarnate in human flesh-embodied spirit. Spirit gives life to spirit. According to Rohr, "... [O]ur core nature is a unique shaping of divine Spirit energy...."[21] According to Paul in his Letter to the Romans, the Spirit who enables us to cry, "Abba!" "Father!" bears witness with our spirit that we are children of God (Rom 8:16). In other words, Spirit outpours itself into spirit; spirit is infused with Spirit. That is why spirituality is a way of living spirit connected to Spirit. "Over time each of us weaves a unique story of responsiveness to the Holy Spirit invitations ...," according to Rohr.[22] According to Paul, "... [W]e speak ... in words not taught by human wisdom but taught by the Spirit, interpreting spiritual things to those who are spiritual" (1 Cor 2:13). That is also why Paul tells the Galatians, "Live by the Spirit ... (Gal 5:16).

We are surrounded by Spirit. We are immersed in Spirit. I am coining a new word here: panenpneumanism; it means *all is in the Spirit*! The psalmist asks the LORD, "Where can I go from your spirit? Or where can I flee from your presence?" (Ps 139:7) The answer is, obviously, there is no place to escape Spirit. Another such question comes from the HB (OT) book of Ecclesiastes: "Who knows whether the human spirit goes upward and the spirit of animals goes downward to the earth?" (Eccl 3:21) The answer: No one knows. "... [T]he spirit of the Lord has filled the world, and that which holds all things together knows what is said," writes the author of the OT (A) book of Wisdom (1:7). There is no clear division between Spirit and spirit; Spirit is interpenetrating spirit. Just as all things are a part of God (panentheism) and nothing is apart from God, so are human spirits a part of Spirit (panenpneumanism) and nothing is apart from Spirit.[23]

We spirits are so immersed in Spirit that Paul can tell the Corinthians: "To one is given through the Spirit the utterance of wisdom, and to another the utterance of knowledge according to the same Spirit, to another faith by the same Spirit, to another gifts of healing by the one Spirit, to another the working of miracles, to another prophecy, to another the discernment of spirits, to another various kinds of tongues, to another

20. Ibid., 54–55.
21. Rohr, "Listening."
22. Ibid.
23. Shapiro, "Roadside Assistance," 48.

the interpretation of tongues. All these are activated by one and the same Spirit, who allots to each one individually just as the Spirit chooses" (1 Cor. 12:9–11). "Once we know that the entire physical world around us, all of creation, is both the hiding place and the revelation place for [Spirit], this world becomes home, safe, enchanted, offering grace to any who look deeply," states Rohr.[24] "God seems to have chosen to manifest the invisible in what we call the 'visible,' so that all things visible are the revelation of God's endlessly diffusive spiritual energy," states Rohr.[25] This is why the author of the Letter to the Hebrews can write that Christ offered himself without blemish to God through the eternal Spirit (Heb 9:14). The human Jesus' spirit was connected to Spirit, just like our spirits are connected to Spirit.

Sheed quotes Julian of Norwich: "I saw no difference between God and our substance but as if it was all God—my understanding took it that our substance is in God, that is to say that God is God and our substance is a creature of God."[26] With a bit of tweaking, we can adapt Julian's words: We see no difference between Spirit and our spirit but as it if was all Spirit—our understanding took it that our spirit is in God, that is to say that Spirit is Spirit and our spirit is a creature of Spirit! In the RM, we pray that following what others have taught by the divine Spirit may enable us to stay firm in our faith[27] and remain on the same spiritual path.[28]

---

24. Rohr, "A Cosmic Notion."
25. Ibid., *Universal Christ*, 17.
26. Sheed, *Knowing God*, 155.
27. "Common of Pastors," II. For a Bishop, 1, Collect, 1074; "Common of Doctors of the Church," 1, Collect, 1088.
28. "Proper of Saints," St. Louis Grignion de Montfort, April 28, Collect, 851.

The Roman Missal and Spirituality

Throughout this book, I have incorporated liturgical Mass texts from *The Roman Missal* and the *Order of Confirmation* that echo Scripture texts. I've done this to demonstrate how Roman Catholics pray Scripture and how Scripture informs prayer. This is liturgical spirituality. Shapiro writes, "Grammar aside, 'spirituality' is a verb: a progressive stripping away of the conditioning that blinds you to the truest fact of your existence: you are a happening of God, YHVH (Exodus 3:15, from the Hebrew verb 'to be'), the Happening happening as all happening."[29] Shapiro continues: "Because spirituality is progressive, I prefer to speak of a maturing rather than a mature spirituality. Spirituality isn't fixed but fluid, not a final 'aha' but a recurring 'wow.'"[30] Spirit is always attempting to connect to spirit in order to continue its development; in Shapiro's words, it is always happening. He states: "A maturing spirituality is active in the world. Knowing the unity of self and other in and as the Happening that is God precludes spiritual narcissism. Or, to put it differently, a maturing spirituality of Self precludes a selfish spirituality of ego or tribe."[31]

Because we are made in God's image and likeness (Gen 1:26) and because he breathed into our nostrils the breath of life (Gen 2:7), we spirits are made to share God's Spirit. Thus, image becomes likeness. We spirits have an innate capacity for transcendence, for Spirit. The (Holy) Spirit connects to (human) spirit and waits for the response that will transform spirit into Spirit. That is why we call the process spirituality. According to John 3:6, what is born of Spirit is spirit. Walsh refers to this as "the spiritual current."[32] Living with spirit connected to Spirit is a never ending "spiritual boot camp," according to Walsh.[33] The OC refers to the process of spirituality as being "spiritually fit."[34]

We begin with our own experience of the human spirit. "Because God is a spirit, we take our own spirit as a starting point."[35] We first experience spirit while in school—school spirit—through yelling, shouting, singing, forming human waves at football, basketball, and baseball games.

29. Shapiro, "Roadside Assistance," 47.
30. Ibid.
31. Ibid., 50.
32. Walsh, *Chasing Mystery*, 47.
33. Ibid., 48.
34. OC, par. 6.
35. Sheed, *Knowing God*, 204.

While we may not articulate it, we feel a part of something that is much bigger than we are individually. Sheed says, "Spirit is the being which has no parts. . . . A part is any element in a being that is not the whole of it."[36] Sheed says that "a partless being does not occupy space."[37] The experience of intangible, but visible, school spirit makes us realize that we are but a part of something that is greater than we are. And while "a spiritual being is strictly unimaginable,"[38] we find metaphors and similes to use—the crowd was wild, the cheerleaders were crazy, the team played hard—in order to communicate to others the experience of school spirit, which unknown to many is spirituality. We do exactly the same thing when Spirit connects to spirit; the biblical metaphors and similes—breath, air, wind, water, dove, etc.—and the modern metaphors and similes—electricity, fish in water, sound, gravity, space, etc.—assist us in plumbing the depths of a spirituality of Spirit and spirit, transforming us step by step throughout our lives.

This Book

Title

The title of this book is *What is Born of the Spirit is Spirit*. As already indicated, the title comes from John's Gospel (3:6). This book provides reflections on all Scripture texts associated with (Holy) Spirit and (human) spirit in the HB (OT), the OT (A), and the CB (NT). Besides the short introduction to the study of the Spirit, called pneumatology, various biblical aspects of Spirit and spirit are explored in one hundred five entries divided into nine chapters.

The subtitle of this book is *A Biblical Spirituality of Spirit*. While much more will be said about biblical spirituality below, the subtitle does

---

36. Ibid., 67.
37. Ibid., 68.
38. Ibid.

not attempt to present a systematic, singular biblical spirituality of Spirit or spirit; it presents the variety of ways biblical authors have been inspired to imagine ways to present that which cannot be pictured: Spirit and spirit.

Using This Book

This book is designed to be used by individuals for private study and prayer and by ministers for study, prayer, and preaching. The goal of this book is to foster the development of biblical spirituality which gets its very name from Spirit.

An five-part exercise is offered for the entries in all nine chapters.

1. **Title**: A one- to four-word title is given to the entry. Not only does the title give focus to the entry, but it imitates *Lectio Divina* (Divine or Sacred Reading), the practice of reading a biblical passage and choosing a word from it for reflection, meditation, and prayer. *Lectio Divina* promotes communion with God through reflection on God's Word (Jesus Christ) and God's word (Bible). Traditionally, *Lectio Divina* has four separate steps: read, reflect, journal/meditate, and pray or contemplate. Kelly says that "*Lectio Divina* was first established by St. Benedict in the sixth century and formalized by the Carthusians in the twelfth. It involves four steps: *lectio* (read), *meditatio* (meditation), *oratio* (pray), and *contemplatio* (contemplation).[39] *Lectio Divina*, according to Thornton, "has been practiced monastically for untold centuries and is a profoundly flexible way of *connecting* with a sacred text, being *read* by the text, and then led into quiet compassionate communion."[40] *Lectio Divina* is especially appropriate with inspired biblical texts.

The short title is designed to promote mindfulness. According to Annemarie Scobey:

> Mindfulness is the practice of maintaining a moment-by-moment awareness of thoughts, feelings, the body, and the surrounding environment. A person who tries to be mindful focuses on what he or she senses and feels in the present moment rather than thinking about what might need to be done later or returning to a memory. Mindfulness is the opposite of multitasking. Mindfulness is truly listening, fully tasting, deeply

---

39. Kelly, "Word," 45.
40. Thornton, "*Lectio Intima*," 36.

experiencing; it's taking our feelings as they come and not burying them or pushing them away.[41]

2. **Scripture**: Since the focus of the entry is found in the title, a verse or two from a Scripture passage under consideration is presented that illustrates the focus. The traditional Benedictine practice of *Lectio Divina*, according to Kelly, is "reading the passage slowly four times, each time with a slightly different focus." Then, one waits "for the action of the Holy Spirit to illuminate [one's] mind as [one] ponders the passage."[42]

3. **Reflection**: The Scripture passage is followed by a two-paragraph reflection on the biblical passage and its understanding in conjunction with other similar biblical verses. The reflection "aims to stimulate thoughts rather than to banish them and sees deep understanding as a way to heighten a personal relationship with God."[43] Throughout the reflections, the masculine pronoun for God, LORD, LORD God, Spirit, etc. is used. The author is well aware that God and Spirit are neither male nor female, but in order to avoid the repetition of nouns over and over again, he employs male pronouns, as they are also used in most biblical translations.

4. **Journal/Meditation**: The reflection is followed by a question for journaling and/or personal meditation. The question functions as a guide for personal appropriation of spirituality, thus leading the reader into journaling and/or personal prayer. The journal/meditation question is designed to foster a process of actively applying the reflection to one's life and further development of it. Kelly says, ". . . [C]ontemplation means making the [Scripture] passage [one's] own by writing about it in the margins, in [one's] prayer journal. . . ."[44] The question gets one started; where the journal/meditation goes cannot be predetermined. It may be a single statement or an idea with which one lingers for a few minutes, a few hours, or a few days. Such contemplation has no end; the reader decides when he or she has finished his or her exploration because he or she needs to attend to other things. People who like to journal—written or electronic—will find the question appropriate for that activity.

According to Scobey:

---

41. Scobey, "Keep Prayer in Mind," 43.
42. Kelly, "Word," 46.
43. Ibid.
44. Ibid.

> Meditation involves quieting the mind and heart. It is a time of focusing our attention on a sacred word or on our breath; a time of letting our thoughts pass by, without holding onto them or entering into them. It is a time of deep awareness.... A common theme ... is silence and stillness. Contemplation, a cousin of meditation, was explained by St. Gregory the Great in the sixth century as "resting in God." St. Gregory went on to explain that in this "resting," the mind and heart are not so much seeking God as beginning to experience God's actual presence. The reduction of action and thought, according to St. Gregory, allows the person practicing contemplation to sustain [his or her] consent to God's presence. In other words—without action and thought, less gets in the way of experiencing God.[45]

"Contemplation is the highest expression of [human] intellectual and spiritual life," Rohr quotes Merton as saying.[46] "It is spiritual wonder. It is spontaneous awe at the sacredness of life, of being. It is gratitude for life, for awareness, and for being. It is a vivid realization of the fact that life and being in us proceed from an invisible, transcendent, and infinitely abundant Source."[47] In this book that Source is Spirit connecting to spirit. Contemplation is the inspired word echoing in us.

"Every development in contemplation reveals more and more of the mystery of silence and the importance of receptivity over effort, especially in prayer," writes Rohr.[48] Before we can receive the Spirit into our spirit, we must enter into silence. "Silence leads to stillness; stillness leads to surrender."[49] According to Rohr, contemplation occurs when our interior silence turns into the awareness of divine presence, spiritual presence, Spirit-presence. "Always," he writes, "contemplation requires attentiveness to the Spirit of God."[50] Thus, meditation, according to Rohr is "any act habitually entered into with our whole heart as a way of awakening and sustaining a more interior meditative awareness of the present moment."[51] In his *The Universal Christ*, Rohr writes, "Contemplation is

---

45. Scobey, "Keep Prayer in Mind,," 43–44.
46. Rohr, "Knowing Our Source."
47. Ibid.
48. Ibid., "Perceiving Reality."
49. Ibid.
50. Ibid., "Connecting to the Eternal."
51. Ibid., "Sustaining Awareness."

waiting patiently for the gaps to be filled in, and it does not insist on quick closure or easy answers."[52]

5. **Prayer**: A prayer concludes the exercise and summarizes the original word in the title, which was illustrated by the Scripture, explored in the reflection, and served as the foundation for the journal/meditation exercise.

True prayer, according to Rohr requires openness of heart, mind, and body. "Those who can keep all three spaces open at the same time will know the Presence they need to know. That's the only prerequisite for true prayer. People who can simply be present will know what they need to know—the Presence that connects everything to everything."[53] In this book, we have named that Presence Spirit.

Through this process of prayer with the focus on the Spirit connecting to spirit, the reader will come to a deeper knowledge of and a closer relationship with God. Sheed reminds us, "God is not a problem to be solved, not even a solution to be admired, but a reality to be possessed, contemplated, conversed with, loved, enjoyed—this is fullness of living."[54] In the pages that follow, I do not attempt to solve any problems or admire any solutions. I hope to awaken the reader's spirit to Spirit so that he or she can contemplate it, converse with it, love it, and enjoy the fullness of its divine life.

According to Kelly, "*Lectio Divina* teaches that not only can a [biblical] text become part of us, any experience in our daily lives might reveal the voice of God if we just learn to listen."[55] As you let this book guide you into deeper experiences of Spirit connecting to spirit and reflect on these experiences, listen to the Spirit inspiring your spirit, thoughts, desires, promptings, etc. Rohr writes, "If something comes toward you with grace and can pass through you and toward others with grace, you can trust it as the voice of God."[56] He adds, "We must listen to what is supporting us. We must listen to what is encouraging us. We must listen to what is urging us. We must listen to what is alive in us."[57] In the Bible we find great characters, prophets, and ordinary people whose spirits are directed by

---

52. Ibid., *Universal Christ*, 8.
53. Ibid., "Open Heart, Mind, and Body."
54. Sheed, *Knowing God*, 10.
55. Kelly, "Word," 46.
56. Rohr, *Universal Christ*, 88.
57. Ibid., 88–89.

the Spirit. What is true of biblical times remains true today. Our spirits are connected to Spirit, the source of all divine life!

Mark G. Boyer
Pentecost Sunday 2019

1

God and Spirit

Spirit in Spirit 1

Scripture: O LORD, "Where can I go from your spirit? Or where can I flee from your presence?" (Ps 139:7)

Reflection: The singer of Psalm 139 stops after six verses of expressions about how the LORD fully knows him or her through actions, thoughts, lifestyle, and speech to ask two key questions: "Where can I go from your spirit? . . . [W]here can I flee from your presence?" (Ps 139:7) Our spirits are surrounded by Spirit. We exist within God's Spirit. We cannot escape from God presence either in heaven, the world above, or in Sheol, the world below (Ps 139:8), and certainly not on the earth, the world in between the other two. We cannot know "whether the human spirit goes upward and the spirit of animals goes downward to the earth" (Eccl 3:21). According to the OT (A) book of Wisdom, ". . . [T]he spirit of the Lord has filled the world . . ." (Wis 1:7a). Since we, spirit, live in the world, we exist within, we breathe in, we live in God's Spirit. The RM expresses this idea as being moved by the divine Spirit.[1]

The fact of the matter is that we, spirit, desire a deeper connection to Spirit. Some of us watch the last dots of darkness be blotted out by the first streaks of light in the eastern sky. Sitting or standing we get caught

---

1. "Common of Pastors," II. For a Bishop, 1, Collect, 1074; "Common of Doctors of the Church," 1, Collect, 1088.

up in the beautifully streaked beginning of a new day, and without even speaking a word we know that spirit has been touched by Spirit. According to the psalmist, the darkness is not dark to the LORD; "the night is as bright as the day, for darkness is as light to [him]" (Ps 139:12). These words are also applicable to gazing at the western streaked sky at sunset as the last dots of light disappear and all is enveloped in darkness. Caught up in that singly, solitary moment, we feel our spirit connected to the Spirit. We are surrounded by Spirit, and we know Spirit has touched spirit deeply and profoundly. The Spirit has come near.[2]

Journal/Meditation: When have you most recently been aware of your spirit being moved by Spirit? Narrate the experience.

Prayer: You formed my innermost self, O LORD, knitting me together in my mother's womb and filling me with spirit. Awaken me day by day to the presence of your Spirit, with whom you live now and forever. Amen.

Sent from on High

Scripture: "Who has learned your counsel, [O God,] unless you have given wisdom and sent your holy spirit from on high?" (Wis 9:17)

Reflection: In the world of biblical composition, the presupposition was that there are three levels: the heavens, the earth, and the underworld. Because each designates a place where there is life—God lives above the heavens, people live on the earth, and the dead live in Sheol—God sends his Spirit from the heavens—from on high according to the OT (A) book of Wisdom—to people on the earth. This same idea is reflected in Luke's Gospel in the CB (NT). The Lukan Jesus states, "[T]he heavenly Father give[s] the Holy Spirit to those who ask him" (Luke 11:13). Similarly, Paul tells the elders of the church of Ephesus to keep watch over all the flock "of which the Holy Spirit has made [them] overseers" (Acts 20:28). In the CB (NT), the best statement that aligns with the one found in the book of Wisdom is located in John's Gospel. The Johannine Jesus tells his disciples, ". . . [T]he Holy Spirit, whom the Father will send in my name, will teach you everything, and remind you of all that I have said to you" (John 14:26).

Biblically, the Spirit is sent by God the Father in heaven to connect to the spirit of those who inhabit the earth. This is the way that people

---

2. OC, par. 35; A, Collect, par. 58.

receive God's counsel, his advice, frequently called discernment. When Spirit connects to spirit, something in a person's life that is not very clear becomes obvious, something not understood becomes knowledge, something not clearly distinguished from something else becomes apparent. Should I take the job offer? Should I move to a new city? Should I propose marriage? Should I buy the car I looked over yesterday? Should I buy the house I toured last weekend? When such questions present themselves to us, why not consult God on high spirit to Spirit? You may be surprised by the answer you receive!

Journal/Meditation: Most recently, when have you consulted God spirit to Spirit? About what did you consult God? What counsel did you receive?

Prayer: Heavenly Father, send your Spirit to connect to my spirit that I may know your will and do it. Through your Spirit, teach me everything that I need to see, understand, and distinguish. Hear me in the name of Jesus Christ, your Son, now and forever. Amen.

Spirit is Life

Scripture: "When you send forth your spirit, [O LORD, your works] are created; and you renew the face of the ground." (Ps 104:30)

Reflection: When Spirit is sent to spirit, the result is life. Psalm 104 references this fact in terms of ongoing creation and the renewal of life that ensues. A similar idea is expressed in a song by Judith in the OT (A) book that bears her name: "Let all your creatures serve you, [O Lord,] for you spoke, and they were made. You sent forth your spirit, and it formed them . . ." (Jdt 16:14). Likewise, creation is the subject of Elihu's first speech to Job: "The spirit of God has made me, and the breath of the Almighty gives me life" (Job 33:4). All of these references are meant to echo the fertile wind from God sweeping over the waters in the HB (OT) book of Genesis (1:2). The RM identifies the wind in Genesis with the Spirit, who, at the first moments of creation, hovered over the waters.[3] In Hebrew, *ruach* is the word for breath, spirit, and wind.

In the Greek language of the CB (NT), *pneuma* is the word for breath, spirit, and wind. This leads Paul in his Letter to the Romans to declare, ". . . [T]he Spirit is life . . ." (Rom 8:10). The Spirit of God gives life to our mortal bodies (Rom 8:11). Living according to the Spirit means

---

3. "Easter Sunday," pars. 44, 46.

we live abundantly (Rom 8:13). In his First Letter to the Corinthians, the apostle presents the first man, Adam, as the one who received the breath of life from God. However, the second man, Christ, who came from heaven, became a life-giving spirit (1 Cor 15:45, 47). Every breath we take and every bit of wind we feel is Spirit connecting to our spirit, giving us life, filling our sails, and giving us a hint of resurrection life to come.

Journal/Meditation: Stop for a few minutes and become aware of your breath, both inhaling and exhaling. Now raise your consciousness to awareness that you are breathing divine Spirit that enlivens your spirit. What appreciation for life does this awakening give you?

Prayer: O LORD, how manifold are all your works, which you have made in your wisdom. Continue to send forth your Spirit to recreate me every second and to renew the face of the earth. May you always rejoice in my spirit, as I praise you for my breath now and forever. Amen.

Spirit Gives Life

Scripture: Jesus said to his disciples, "It is the spirit that gives life . . . ." (John 6:63)

Reflection: Long before the Johannine Jesus declares that the Spirit gives life, Paul tells the Galatians, ". . . [I]f you sow to the Spirit, you will reap eternal life from the Spirit" (Gal 6:8). Using the planting-of-grain metaphor, the apostle tells his readers and us that we reap whatever we sow. The author of the Letter of James declares that "the body without the spirit is dead" (Jas 2:26). The First Letter of Peter applies this idea to Jesus: "He was put to death in the flesh, but made alive in the spirit" (1 Pet 3:18b). Before the author of the First Letter of Peter and the Letter of James applied the words to Jesus about spirit giving life, the author of the Second Book of Maccabees applied them to a certain Razis, who calls upon the Lord of life and spirit to give them back to him again after he dies (2 Macc 14:46).

Like this author, you may find yourself asking Job's question posed to Bildad the Shuhite: "With whose help have you uttered words, and whose spirit has come forth from you?" (Job 26:4) We answer using the words of the Creed found in the RM: "I believe in the Holy Spirit, the Lord, the giver of life . . . ."[4] The members of the church, established as a

---

4. "Order of Mass," par. 18.

holy city, are given life by the Spirit.[5] Life comes from Spirit sent to spirit. In other words, the Spirit is the great vivifying principle. Pure spirit is pure Spirit. We experience our spirit being vivified by Spirit when we stand beside ourselves, when we are drawn to an awareness of all things' spirit-animated by the same Spirit, when someone's love for us is poured into us and our love for the other is poured back into him or her.

Journal/Meditation: What has been your most recent experience of Spirit giving life to your spirit? Narrate the occasion. What was the experience of Spirit-spirit life like?

Prayer: Father, you give life to everything created through the Spirit. Grant me the grace to sow in the Spirit throughout my life that I may reap eternal life from the Spirit in the next life. Here this prayer in the name of Jesus now and forever. Amen.

Spirit-Breath

Scripture: Elihu son of Barachel the Buzite answered: "... [T]ruly it is the spirit in a mortal, the breath of the Almighty, that makes for understanding." (Job 32:8)

Reflection: As already indicated above, the Hebrew word *ruach* can mean breath, spirit, and wind. In the HB (OT) book of Job, Elihu defines spirit in people as the breath of God. In the same HB (OT) book, Job has already declared that "as long as [his] breath is in [him] and the spirit of God is in [his] nostrils" (Job 27:3), he will not speak falsehood or utter deceit. The OT (A) book of Wisdom states that God breathes a living spirit into people (Wis 15:11c). However, it is the prophet Isaiah, who declares that God, the LORD, "who created the heavens and stretched them out, who spread out the earth and what comes from it, ... gives breath to the people upon it and spirit to those who walk in it" (Isa 42:5). Thus, to think about spirit and Spirit is simultaneously to think about breath, or to become aware of our breath is simultaneously to become aware of our spirit united to Spirit.

Breathing is an act of inspiration, breathing in of Spirit. Because we are not always conscious of our breath, most spiritual exercises begin with breathing exercises. We focus on becoming conscious of inhaling and exhaling in order to quiet our minds. By keeping them from running

---

5. "Ritual Masses," X. For the Dedication of a Church and an Altar, 1. For the Dedication of a Church, Preface, 1222–24.

today's errands, tomorrow's grocery list, or the weekend chores, we breathe in and out. Not only is this breath a gift of the LORD God, it is "the breath of life" which makes us living beings (cf. Gen 2:7); in other words, it is Spirit sharing spirit with mortals. It is the very Spirit of God that we inhabit, like a fish inhabiting the ocean. It's not surround-sound; it is surround-breath, surround-spirit, surround-Spirit. Becoming aware of breath is a stimulus to creativity in the same way as the Spirit is God's inspiration and life-gift to creation.

Journal/Meditation: When have you recently experienced the breath of God inspiring you, guiding you, assisting you in discernment of any kind? What role did awareness of your own breathing play in your experience?

Prayer: LORD God, you created the heavens and stretched them over the earth and all that lives upon its ground and in its seas. You give breath to me and spirit to all people who walk upon the earth. Fill me with ongoing gift of your Spirit now and forever. Amen.

Spirit of the LORD

Scripture: "The spirit of the LORD shall rest on [the shoot from the stump of Jesse], the spirit of wisdom and understanding, the spirit of counsel and might, the spirit of knowledge and the fear of the LORD." (Isa 11:2)

Reflection: In the HB (OT), the Spirit is often referred to as the Spirit of the LORD. In the above verse from the prophet Isaiah, the hope is expressed for a Davidic descendant after the Babylonian exile to rule the southern kingdom of Judah with the Spirit of God resting on him. In later and separate entries we will examine the resting-upon metaphor and the spirit of wisdom, understanding, counsel, might, knowledge, and fear mentioned by Isaiah. What concerns us here is the existence of the Spirit of God. All the Spirit's other biblical activities will be examined later. In order to emphasize God's supremacy, Isaiah asks, "Who has directed the spirit of the LORD, or as his counselor has instructed him?" (Isa 40:13) The prophet Zechariah also presents God's all-powerful Spirit when he writes about his vision of an angel, who tells him: "This is the word of the LORD to Zerubbabel [, governor of Judah]: Not by might, nor by power, but by my spirit, says the LORD of hosts" (Zech 4:6). In the CB (NT), the author of the Letter to the Hebrews refers to the Spirit of God as "the eternal Spirit" (Heb 9:14).

In the Apostles' Creed in the RM, we declare belief in the Holy Spirit.[6] Likewise, when renewing baptismal promises during the Easter Vigil and before Confirmation, we express belief in the Hoy Spirit, the Lord and giver of life.[7] Likewise, in the Niceno-Constantinopolitan Creed, also in the RM, we not only declare belief in the Holy Spirit, but declare that the Spirit, named the Lord, proceeds from the Father and Son.[8] This last statement means that as one of the persons of the co-equal and co-eternal Trinity, the Holy Spirit is consubstantial with the Father and the Son,[9] that is, the Spirit is of the same substance as the Father and the Son. Thus, it is appropriate to refer to the Spirit of the LORD in the same way as calling Jesus God's Son. The metaphor Father-Son used to describe the relationship of two members of the Trinity is based on human experience. The metaphor Spirit-spirit used to describe the relationship of the Spirit of the Lord with the human spirit is based on the human experience that leaves us inspired or inspirited.

Journal/Meditation: What does saying "I believe in the Holy Spirit" mean to you? What metaphors do you use to describe the Spirit-spirit metaphor?

Prayer: Father, I believe in the Holy Spirit, the giver of life, who proceeds from you and your Son, Jesus Christ. Fill my spirit with your Spirit that I may be inspired to do your will now and forever. Amen.

Paraclete

Scripture: Jesus said to his disciples, ". . . I will ask the Father, and he will give you another Advocate, to be with you forever. This is the Spirit of truth . . . ." (John 14:16–17)

Reflection: The Greek word that is translated above as Advocate is *paracletos*—transliterated as Paraclete and unique to Johannine literature. The Greek word "means the person called to the side of one in need of assistance, particularly in legal processes; but it does not signify a

---

6. "Order of Mass," par. 19.
7. "Easter Sunday," par. 55; OC, pars. 23, 40.
8. "Order of Mass," par. 18; OC, pars. 30, 47.
9. CCC, par. 685.

professional advocate."[10] In John's Gospel, Jesus identifies the Spirit as the Paraclete. ". . . [T]he Advocate, the Holy Spirit, whom the Father will send in my name, will teach you everything, and remind you of all that I have said to you," the Johannine Jesus says to his disciples (John 14:26). Later, he adds, "When the Advocate comes, whom I will send to you from the Father, the Spirit of truth who comes from the Father, he will testify on my behalf. . . . [I]f I do not go away, the Advocate will not come to you; but if I go, I will send him to you" (John 15:26; 16:7). Other biblical translations of the Greek *paracletos* include Comforter, Counselor, Helper, Intercessor, Strengthener, and Standby. It is important to note here that the First Letter of John identifies the Paraclete as Jesus Christ (1 John 2:1); thus, John 14:16 presents the Johannine Jesus telling his disciples about another Paraclete.

The use of Paraclete as another name for the Holy Spirit is also found in the RM and in the OC. The Paraclete is described as proceeding from the Lord.[11] In the OC, the prayer said while the bishop (and priests) extends his hands over those to be confirmed asks God to send the Holy Spirit, the Paraclete, upon them.[12] In other words, the bishop (and priests) is calling upon God to send the Spirit, the Advocate, to stand by the side of those in need of assistance. We experience this Comforter when another consoles us with a pat on the back. We experience this Counselor when another speaks words that propel us in a new direction. We experience this Helper when another shares our chores. We experience this Intercessor when another speaks for us. We experience this Strengthener when another assists us in our weakness. And we experience this Standby when another supports our cause. No matter how we experience the Paraclete, it is the Holy Spirit.

Journal/Meditation: When have you most recently experienced the Holy Spirit as Comforter, Counselor, Helper, Intercessor, Strengthener, and Standby?

Prayer: Heavenly Father, send the Paraclete to me that he may be revealed as your Comforter, Counselor, Helper, Intercessor, Strengthener, and Standby. He lives and reigns with you and your Son, Jesus Christ, as the Holy Spirit now and forever. Amen.

---

10. McKenzie, *Dictionary*, 636; CCC, par. 692.

11. "Ritual Masses," 4. For the Conferral of Confirmation, C, Collect, 1134; "Votive Masses," 9. The Holy Spirit, B, Collect, 1341; OC, Collect, par. 60.

12. OC, pars. 25, 42.

Spirit Seeks Spirit 1

Scripture: "The hand of the LORD came upon me [, Ezekiel], and he brought me out by the spirit of the LORD and set me down in the middle of a valley; it was full of bones. Then he said to me, 'Prophesy to the breath, prophesy, mortal, and say to the breath: Thus says the Lord GOD: Come from the four winds, O breath, and breathe upon these slain, that they may live.' I prophesied as he commanded me, and the breath came into them, and they lived . . . ." (Ezek 37:1, 9–10)

Reflection: Because *ruach* can mean breath, air, wind, or spirit, other biblical translations often record the Lord GOD telling the prophet Ezekiel to prophesy to the spirit, begging him to send the breath of spirit from the four winds to bring back to life the bones scattered in the middle of a valley. Repeatedly, Ezekiel records his experiences of God's Spirit seeking his spirit. When God speaks to him, he notes that a spirit enters into him (Ezek 2:2; 3:24), or the spirit lifts him up (Ezek 3:12, 14; 8:3; 11:1, 24; 43:5), or the spirit of the LORD falls upon him (Ezek 11:5), or the spirit of the LORD is put within him (Ezek 37:14). In a similar vein, the narrator of the story about Susanna in the OT (A) book of Daniel states that "God stirred up the holy spirit of a young lad named Daniel" (Sus 1:45 [Dan 13:45]). The LORD stirs up spirit because, according to the prophet Zechariah, he "formed the human spirit within" (Zech 12:1) and, according to the prophet Malachi, "[b]oth flesh and spirit are his" (Mal 2:15). The HB (OT) book of Proverbs says it best: "The human spirit is the lamp of the LORD, searching every inmost part" (Prov 20:27).

God's Spirit is recorded as seeking the human spirit in the CB (NT), too. In his First Letter to the Corinthians, Paul states that "the Spirit searches everything, even the depths of God" (1 Cor 2:10). Then he asks his readers, "For what human being knows what is truly human except the human spirit that is within?" (Cor 2:11a) Then, he concludes, "So also no one comprehends what is truly God's except the Spirit of God" (1 Cor 2:11b). According to the author of the Letter of James: "God yearns jealously for the spirit that he has made to dwell in us" (Jas 4:5). The goal of spirituality is to "live in the spirit as God does" (1 Pet 4:6). The author of the First Letter of John presents a guideline to determine if one is living in the Spirit that has sought our spirit: "By this you know the Spirit of God: every spirit that confesses that Jesus Christ has come in the flesh is from God, and every spirit that does not confess Jesus is not from God" (1 John 4:2–3).

Journal/Meditation: Have you ever experienced the Spirit as entering you, lifting you up, falling upon you, put within you, stirring you, searching you, or yearning jealously for you? How would you describe your experience of the Spirit seeking your spirit? What might be other ways to describe Spirit seeking spirit?

Prayer: Lord GOD, from the four winds send the breath of your Spirit into me that I may live eternally. Your Spirit yearns jealously to enter into me, to lift me up, and stir me up now and forever. Amen.

Spirit in Spirit 2

Scripture: "For though I am absent in body, yet I am with you in spirit . . . ." (Col 2:5)

Reflection: The author of the Letter to the Colossians, writing in the name of Paul after he was dead, presents one of the results of Spirit in spirit. The author of Colossians could present Paul writing that even though he was not present, he was, nevertheless, with his readers in spirit. How? The one divine Spirit connects with and together all other spirits. Thus, even when absent bodily, one is, nevertheless, present spiritually. In his Letter to the Romans, Paul specifically tells his readers that they "are in the Spirit, since the Spirit of God dwells" in them (Rom 8:9). John of Patmos, the narrator of the CB (NT) book of Revelation explains that he "was in the spirit on the Lord's day" (Rev 1:10), that he "was in the spirit" (Rev 4:2), and that he was "carried . . . away in the spirit" (Rev 17:3, 10); he also could have said that his spirit was in the Spirit every day. In other words, Spirit forms a world-wide web of spirits.

Spirit in spirit is a theme that permeates John's Gospel in the CB (NT). The Johannine authors refer to it as "in spirit and truth" (John 4:23). Because "God is spirit," he must be worshiped "in spirit and truth" (John 4:24), the Johannine Jesus tells a Samaritan woman. Later, the Johannine Jesus identifies the Paraclete as "the Spirit of truth" (John 14:17; 16:13; 1 John 4:6c; 5:6b) and "the Spirit of truth who comes from the Father" (John 15:26). Spirituality is the practice of a way of living your life aware that your spirit is in the Spirit, in the Spirit of truth. Through your spirit you are always connected to Spirit, the LORD, the giver of life. No matter whether you are bodily present are not, you are spiritually present to all others in the web.

Journal/Meditation: Make a list of people with whom you are in the Spirit. For each, answer this question: In what specific way are you present to each person in spirit while not being physically present to each?

Prayer: Holy Spirit, you are the Lord, the giver of life, and the Spirit of truth. Keep my spirit connected to you that all I say and do may be said and done in spirit and in truth. Grant my prayer in the name of Jesus Christ now and forever. Amen.

Through Spirit

Scripture: "... [T]hrough the Spirit, by faith, we eagerly wait for the hope of righteousness." (Gal 5:5)

Reflection: In Pauline thought, all those whose spirits are connected to Spirit long for the fullness of God. Paul refers to this longing as the hope of righteousness, hope for adoption, hope for redemption (Rom 8:18–25). Spirit connected to spirit gives us a foretaste of what is to come. "... [T]he one who raised the Lord Jesus will raise us also with Jesus, and will bring us with you into his presence," the apostle writes to the Corinthians (2 Cor 4:14). In other words, "we have the same spirit of faith" (2 Cor 4:13), that is, the same capacity to believe and wait in hope through the Spirit. The CCC states that the Spirit is the first to awaken faith in us and to communicate to us new life.[13] The RM refers to this awakening as the spirit of faith.[14]

The OC explains that the Spirit conforms people more fully to Christ so that they build up his body in faith.[15] We know by faith, states OC, that the Spirit is received.[16] It is through the Spirit that God raises up people to awaken others to seek deeper connections of their spirit to the Spirit[17] in the hope that God will one day raise them from the dead. For it was through the Holy Spirit that God raised Christ from the dead.[18] And

---

13. CCC, par. 684.

14. "Ritual Masses," X. For the Dedication of a Church and an Altar, 1. For the Dedication of a Church, (a) Eucharistic Prayer I Commemoration, 1226.

15. OC, par. 2.

16. Ibid., pars. 22, 39.

17. "Proper of Saints," St. Teresa of Jesus, October 15, Collect, 970.

18. "Masses for the Dead," B. For Several Deceased Persons or for All the Dead, 5, Prayer after Communion, 1396.

he with the Holy Spirit exists in the glory of God the Father.[19] It is this glory which we hope to share through the Spirit connected to our spirit.

Journal/Meditation: Through the Spirit, who has awakened you to seek a deeper connection of your spirit to the Spirit? How did he or she do it?

Prayer: Holy One, through your Spirit you raised your Son, Jesus Christ, from the dead and seated him in glory at your right hand. Raise up those who can awaken me to a deeper awareness of your Spirit at work in my spirit and grant that I may one day share in the gory of eternal life forever. Amen.

The Lord be with Your Spirit

Scripture: "The Lord be with your spirit." (2 Tim 4:22a)

Reflection: The benediction found at the end of the Second Letter to Timothy is similar to the one found in Paul's Letter to Philemon and his Letter to the Philippians: "The grace of the Lord Jesus Christ be with your spirit" (Phlm 1:25; Phil 4:23). And all of those benedictions are similar to the one found at the end of the Letter to the Galatians: "May the grace of our Lord Jesus Christ be with your spirit, brothers and sisters. Amen" (Gal 6:18). Literally meaning *to speak (dico) well (bene) to*, the benediction at the end of the letters mentioned above is a conveyance of good wishes. They ask for the Lord (not the LORD) Jesus Christ's blessing upon the spirit of those who read the letters. In other words, the writers' wish is that spirit will be touched by Spirit in human hearts (2 Cor 1:22). In his Second Letter to the Corinthians, Paul phrases the same idea this way: "... [Y]ou show that you are a letter of Christ, prepared by us written not with ink but with the Spirit of the living God, not on tablets of stone but on tablets of human hearts" (2 Cor 3:3). In other words, the Spirit of Christ, who lives within people, touches their spirit and is the content of the letter. Who wouldn't want to wish the blessing of Spirit connecting to spirit to others?

In the RM, the minister begins worship of any kind with the same wish: "The Lord be with you." And the worshipers respond: "And with your spirit."[20] This greeting is meant to awaken both minister and worshipers to the presence of the Spirit and the opportunity for spirits to be

---

19. "Order of Mass," par. 8.
20. Ibid., par. 1.

connected to Spirit. This awakening occurs two more times during the celebration of Mass. Before beginning the Eucharistic Prayer, the minister says or sings, "The Lord be with you," and the worshipers respond, "And with your spirit."[21] The third time the minister wishes the Lord Jesus' presence to worshipers and they respond with the same wish for his spirit is the blessing at the end of Mass.[22] Also, there are two occasions when a priest or bishop wishes the Lord Jesus' presence in the heart and on the lips of the deacon in the name of the (Father, Son and) Holy Spirit: before The Easter Proclamation[23] and before the deacon's proclamation of the gospel.[24] In all these benedictions, one person wishes the gift of Spirit to spirit.

Journal/Meditation: Upon whose spirit do you wish the Spirit? How does your wish of Spirit to spirit affect your spirit?

Prayer: O LORD, you are ever-present to your people. Continue to bless my spirit with your Spirit that I may, in turn, share that same Spirit with all I meet. I ask this in the name of Jesus Christ, your Son, who with you, Father, live and reign with the Holy Spirit in perfect Trinity forever and ever. Amen.

Spirit Returned

Scripture: ". . . Jesus, crying with a loud voice, said, 'Father, into your hands, I commend my spirit.'" (Luke 23:46a)

Reflection: In the CB (NT), the author of Luke's Gospel is the first evangelist to write about Spirit returning to spirit. His first statement concerning this is found in the account of the death of the daughter of Jairus (Luke 8:40-42, 49-56). While Luke found this story in Mark's Gospel (5:21-24, 35-43), he adds uniquely that the daughter's "spirit returned" (Luke 8:55); Spirit returned to spirit; she who was dead is now alive. This paves the way for the Lukan Jesus to declare before his death, "Father, into your hands, I commend my spirit" (Luke 23:46a), an almost direct quotation of a verse from Psalm 31: "Into your hand I commit my spirit;

---

21. Ibid., pars. 31, 33-83, 99, 107, 116; "Appendix," Eucharistic Prayers for Reconciliation, I, par. 1; II, par 1; Eucharistic Prayer for Use in Masses for Various Needs, I, par 1; II, par. 1; III, par. 1; IV, par 1.

22. "Order of Mass," pars. 141, 143.

23. "Easter Sunday," par. 18.

24. "Order of Mass," par. 14.

you have redeemed me, O LORD, faithful God" (Ps 31:5). In other words, Jesus returns the Spirit he received at his conception and baptism (about which more will be written below); spirit returns Spirit. Because the author of Luke's Gospel also wrote the Acts of the Apostles, he portrays Stephen, before he dies, returning his spirit to Spirit, saying, "Lord Jesus, receive my spirit" (Acts 7:59). In John's Gospel, the narrator informs the reader that Jesus "bowed his head and gave up his spirit" (John 19:30b); spirit is returned to Spirit.

As indicated above, the idea of returning one's spirit to the God who gave it is found in Psalm 31. It is also found in Psalm 51: "[O God,] [d]o not cast me away from your presence, and do not take your holy spirit from me" (Ps 51:11); should God do this, the person would die. In the HB (OT) book of Job, Elihu explains what would happen if God took back his Spirit: "If he should take back his spirit to himself, and gather to himself his breath, all flesh would perish together, and all mortals return to dust" (Job 34:14). Elihu's vision reverses the account in the HB (OT) book of Genesis in which the LORD God breathes the breath of life into the man and he became a living being (Gen 2:7). The basic idea of returning spirit to Spirit is that life is returned to its Creator, who receives and redeems it.

Journal/Meditation: Whom have you known who died happily by returning his or her spirit to Spirit? How did he or she do this? What scares you about returning spirit to Spirit?

Prayer: Heavenly Father, do not cast me away from your presence, and do not take your Spirit from me. Strengthen me daily to place my spirit into your hands knowing that you have redeemed me, O LORD, faithful God. Amen.

Spirit Seeks Spirit 2

Scripture: "My soul yearns for you in the night [, O LORD], my spirit within me earnestly seeks you." (Isa 26:9a)

Reflection: Just as God's Spirit seeks my spirit, my spirit seeks Spirit. The HB (OT) prophet Isaiah records this sentiment in a song of praise, a verse of which is presented above. It is also found in Hezekiah's psalm recorded in Isaiah: "O Lord, by these things people live, and in all these is the life of my spirit" (Isa 38:16a). The NABRE captures the deeper meaning of this verse in Hezekiah's psalm: "Those live whom the LORD protects; yours is the life of my spirit" (Isa 38:16a). The same idea is presented in what seems to be the voice of Cyrus, King of Persia, who states, ". . . [N]ow the Lord GOD has sent me and his spirit" (Isa 48:16). The HB (OT) book of Second Chronicles is clearer, stating, ". . . [T]he LORD stirred up the spirit of King Cyrus of Persia so that he sent a herald throughout all his kingdom and also declared in a written edict: 'Thus says King Cyrus of Persia: The LORD, the God of heaven, has given me all the kingdoms of the earth, and he has charged me to build him a house at Jerusalem, which is in Judah . . .'" (2 Chr 36:22–23a). In this last instance, after Spirit sought Cyrus's spirit, his spirit sought Spirit in order to respond by authorizing the rebuilding of the temple in Jerusalem.

In the CB (NT), spirit seeking Spirit is expressed in Mary's song in Luke's Gospel. She declares, ". . . [M]y spirit rejoices in God my Savior . . ." (Luke 1:47); in other words, my spirit rejoices in Spirit. This is her response to having had the Spirit come upon her and overshadow her (Luke 1:35). Similarly, in his First Letter to the Corinthians, as we have already noted above, Paul writes: ". . . [T]hese things [that God has prepared for those who love him] God has revealed to us through the Spirit; for the Spirit searches everything, even the depths of God. For what human being knows what is truly human except the human spirit that is within? So also no one comprehends what is truly God's except the Spirit of God. Now we have received not the spirit of the world, but the Spirit that is from God, so that we may understand the gifts bestowed on us by God" (1 Cor 2:10–12). According to Paul, God's Spirit seeks our spirit and inspires our spirit to seek the Spirit, who enables us to understand the things of God.

Journal/Meditation: What understanding of the things of God has your spirit sought and received from Spirit? What understanding of the things of God does your spirit seek and await revelation from the Spirit?

Prayer: O LORD, my spirit yearns for you in the night. O God, my spirit within me earnestly seeks you, who give life to my spirit. Grant that my spirit may never cease to understand your things and receive the revelation of your Spirit, who is Lord, forever and ever. Amen.

2

Spirit as Gift

Gift of Spirit

Scripture: ". . . [I]t is God who establishes us with you in Christ . . . by . . . giving us his Spirit in our hearts as a first installment." (2 Cor 1:22).

Reflection: Because Spirit and spirit are incorporeal and, thus, invisible, the only way to write about them is metaphorical. In his First Letter to the Thessalonians, Paul reminds his readers that God "gives his Holy Spirit" (1 Thess 4:8); the implied metaphor is that God gives the Spirit as a gift. In his Second Letter to the Corinthians, Paul writes about the gift of the Spirit as a first installment or down payment; this gesture of God's good faith in people indicates that he will pay the balance later. Gift implies that the Spirit is free. Later, in the same letter, Paul states that God "has given us the Spirit as a guarantee" (2 Cor 5:5); more free Spirit awaits us. In his second speech in the Acts of the Apostle, Peter emphasizes God's gift when he tells his listeners to repent and be baptized in the name of Jesus Christ and they "will receive the gift of the Holy Spirit" (Acts 2:38). Later, Peter refers to "the Holy Spirit whom God has given to those who obey him" (Acts 5:32) and God's act of "giving . . . the Holy Spirit" (Acts 15:8).

The metaphor of the Holy Spirit being like a gift freely given is found in the RM and in the OC. In the RM, God is asked to preserve the gift of the Holy Spirit which he has endowed in the hearts of believers,[1] just as he gave the Holy Spirit to the apostles.[2] The OC explains: "By this gift of the Holy Spirit the faithful are more fully conformed to Christ and are strengthened with the power to bear witness to Christ . . . ."[3] The ideas that the gift of the Spirit conforms one to Christ and enables him or her to bear witness form a theme that is found throughout the OC.[4] Our emphasis in this reflection is on the metaphor of the Spirit as a freely-given gift. In a world in which many people presume that they must give a gift to a person who gave a gift to them (gift exchange), we may need to revisit the definition of gift as something that is given to somebody freely. In its definition of gift, *Encarta* cautions: "Marketers are fond of the expression *free gift* . . . . But because any *gift* worthy of its name is free, the result of using the two words together is both illogical and exaggerated. The phrase *free gift* should be avoided."[5]

Journal/Meditation: For you, what are the connotations of the metaphor gift for the Spirit? What does God's freely-given gift of Spirit enable you to do?

Prayer: Almighty Father, you gave the gift of your Holy Spirit to the followers of your Son, Jesus Christ. Give me this precious gift that I may be conformed to him and bear witness that you are one God—Father, Son, and Holy Spirit—now and forever. Amen.

Gifts of the Spirit

Scripture: "Now there are varieties of gifts, but the same Spirit; and there are varieties of services, but the same Lord; and there are varieties of activities, but is the same God who activates all them in everyone." (1 Cor 12:4–6)

Reflection: While we will develop in detail the specific gifts of the Spirit later, here it is important to note that the gift of the Spirit in the previous entry is not the same as the gifts of the Spirit in this entry. In

---

1. "Ritual Masses," I. For the Conferral of the Sacraments of Christian Initiation, 4. For the Conferral of Confirmation, C, Prayer over the Offerings, 1134.

2. "Votive Masses," 10. The Blessed Virgin Mary, D, Our Lady, Queen of Apostles, Collect, 1351.

3. OC, par. 2.

4. Ibid., pars. 9, 22, 30, 39, 47, 49, 60.

5. *Encarta*, 751.

chapter 12 of Paul's First Letter to the Corinthians, the apostle explains the varieties of gifts of the Spirit (1 Cor 12:4–10). His point is this: "All these [gifts] are activated by one and the same Spirit, who allots to each one individually just as the Spirit chooses" (1 Cor 12:11). Earlier in the same letter he cautions: "Those who are unspiritual do not receive the gifts of God's Spirit, for they are foolishness to them, and they are unable to understand them because they are spiritually discerned" (1 Cor 2:14). The author of the Letter to the Hebrews echoes Paul's words, writing about God's "gifts of the Holy Spirit, distributed according to his will" (Heb 2:4).

As in the previous entry, the metaphor of the Holy Spirit giving gifts freely is found in the RM and in the OC. In the RM, God is asked to preserve the gifts of the Holy Spirit which he has endowed in the hearts of the faithful.[6] He is also asked to fill his servants with the gifts of the Holy Spirit.[7] Even more specifically, echoing Pauline thought above, are the petitions that the Spirit imbue people powerfully with spiritual gifts[8] and imbue the world with the spirit of Christ.[9] The OC presents the diverse graces, which the Spirit distributes to individuals.[10] It also refers to the abundant gifts which the Spirit pours on people[11] and asks God to preserve those gifts of the Spirit in the hearts of his faithful people.[12]

Journal/Meditation: What abundant gifts have you received from the Spirit? Make a list. After each gift indicate how you have used it.

Prayer: O God, your Spirit bestows an abundance of spiritual gifts upon your people. Give me those gifts, I pray, that I may use them to build up your people, the church, the body of Christ, now and forever. Amen.

---

6. "Ritual Masses," I. For the Conferral of the Sacraments of Christian Initiation, 4. For the Conferral of Confirmation, A, Prayer over the People, 1132.

7. Ibid., VIII. For Religious Profession, 2. For Perpetual Profession, B, Prayer over the Offerings, 1217.

8. "Proper of Time," Easter Time, Thursday of the Seventh Week of Easter, Collect, 442.

9. "Masses and Prayers," 10. For the Laity, Collect, 1257.

10. OC, pars. 22, 29.

11. Ibid., pars. 24, 41.

12. Ibid., pars. 33, 49.

Spirit Poured Out 1

Scripture: "Thus says the LORD who made you, who formed you in the womb and will help you: . . . I will pour my spirit upon your descendants, and my blessing on your offspring." (Isa 44:2a, 3b)

Reflection: A metaphor often employed through some of biblical literature is that of pouring out the Spirit, as can be noted above in the text from the HB (OT) prophet Isaiah. The verb *to pour* means *to make a fluid substance flow in a stream*. When the word *out* is added to pour, it means *to flow in large quantities*. The verb *to outpour* means *to make something flow out quickly*. While the distinctions between pour, pour out, and outpour are subtle, attention is called to the flowing in large quantities of pour out and the flowing out quickly of outpour. Thus, Isaiah writes about "a spirit from on high [being] poured out" (Isa 32:15), and the prophet Ezekiel records the Lord GOD declaring, ". . . I pour out my spirit upon the house of Israel . . ." (Ezek 39:29), while the prophet Joel records the LORD God stating, "I will pour out my spirit on all flesh" (Joel 2:28), and the prophet Zechariah presents the LORD saying, ". . . I will pour out a spirit of compassion and supplication on the house of David and the inhabitants of Jerusalem . . ." (Zech 12:10).

In the CB (NT), the apostle Peter quotes Joel in his post-Pentecost speech. "In the last days it will be, God declares, that I will pour out my Spirit upon all flesh . . . ," states Peter (Acts 2:17a). And in the same speech, he further emphasizes that God has poured out the Holy Spirit (Acts 2:33). The Letter to Titus adds that God has poured out the Spirit richly through Jesus Christ (Titus 3:6). The OC states that it is through Confirmation that the baptized receive the outpouring of the Holy Spirit.[13] It identifies the first outpouring of the Spirit occurring on Pentecost,[14] attributes the Spirit with the pouring of God's love into people's hearts,[15] and identifies Jesus' ministry as pouring out the Spirit.[16] In one prayer in the OC and in the RM, God is asked graciously to pour out the Holy Spirit,[17] and in another to pour the Spirit of love on those confirmed.[18]

---

13. Ibid., par. 1.
14. Ibid., par. 7.
15. Ibid., pars. 22, 39.
16. Ibid., pars. 22, 39.
17. Ibid., pars. 24, 41, 59 (Collect); "Ritual Masses," I. For the Conferral of the Sacraments of Christian Initiation, 4. For the Conferral of Confirmation, B, Collect, 1133.
18. OC, par. 60 (Prayer after Communion); "Ritual Masses," I. For the Conferral of

Thus in various manners we ask God to pour the Spirit on us, like a fluid substance flowing in a stream; to pour out the Spirit on us, like a fluid substance flowing in very large quantities, and to outpour the Spirit, like a fluid substance that flows out very quickly.

Journal/Meditation: Other than those presented above, what associations do you make with pouring, pouring out, and outpouring? Which one best describes your experience with the Spirit?

Prayer: Almighty Father, your pour out your Holy Spirit upon all your sons and daughters in order make them abundant with gifts. Grant that I may witness the outpouring of the same Spirit throughout the world today, tomorrow, and forever. Amen.

Spirit Poured Out 2

Scripture: Thus says the LORD God: "Even on the male and female slaves, in those days, I will pour out my spirit." (Joel 2:29)

Reflection: As already noted above, pouring out indicates the flow of a large quantity and outpouring indicates fast-flowing. Thus, in the above verse from the HB (OT) prophet Joel, the LORD God decides to pour out on slaves a large quantity of Spirit. Eucharistic Prayer for Reconciliation I asks God to pour out the Spirit on the offerings of bread and wine,[19] whereas Reconciliation II asks God to sanctify the gifts of bread and wine by the outpouring of his Spirit.[20] In the RM, the Lord is also asked to pour out the Spirit of his love,[21] to pour out the Holy Spirit,[22] to pour out the gifts of the Holy Spirit,[23] to ensure that the gift of the Spirit

---

the Sacraments of Christian Initiation, 4. For the Conferral of Confirmation, B, Prayer after Communion, 1134.

19. "Appendix," Eucharistic Prayers for Reconciliation I, par. 3.

20. Ibid., Eucharistic Prayers for Reconciliation II, par. 3.

21. "Easter Sunday," par. 67; "Ordinary Time," Second Sunday in Ordinary Time, Prayer after Communion, 462; "Ritual Masses," V. For the Celebration of Marriage, B, Solemn Blessing, 1188.

22. "Pentecost Sunday," par. 7; "Proper of Saints," St. Vincent, January 23, Collect, 809; "Masses and Prayers," I. For Holy Church, 18. For the Evangelization of Peoples, A, Collect, 1279; "Votive Masses," 9. The Holy Spirit, A, Preface, 1339–40; 14. All the Holy Apostles, Prayer over the Offerings, 1359.

23. "Pentecost Sunday," At the Mass during the Day, Collect, 453; "Masses and Prayers," I. For Holy Church, 17. For the Unity of Christians, B, Prayer after Communion, 127; C, Collect, 1277; "Votive Masses," 9. The Holy Spirit, C, Collect, 1344.

poured out on the church retains all its force,[24] to pour into the hearts of a newly married couple the power of the Spirit,[25] to consecrate people to himself through the outpouring of the Spirit,[26] to pour out a spirit of piety and fortitude in the church,[27] to pour out the grace of the Spirit,[28] to engender unity in the diversity of gifts through the Spirit poured out among all the nations,[29] to cleanse hearts through the outpouring of the Spirit,[30] and to pour the delights of the Spirit into the heart's recesses.[31] Finally, in the solemn blessing on days in honor of the Holy Spirit, the first strophe acknowledges God, who was pleased to enlighten the minds of disciples by the outpouring of the Spirit.[32]

While each one of the phrases about the Spirit used in the RM above include the idea of pouring out or outpouring, each of them also is more specific. Asking God to pour out the Spirit of self-sacrificial love differs from asking that the gift of the Spirit poured out on the church retains all its force. Asking the LORD to pour into the hearts of a newly married couple the power of the Spirit differs from asking God to engender unity in the diversity of gifts through the Spirit poured out among all the nations. And the request that God pour the delights of the Spirit into the recesses of people's hearts gives a playful connotation to the verb *to pour*. This metaphor is used in multiple ways to attempt to capture the activity of the Spirit.

Journal/Meditation: Which of the phrases above used in the RM to describe the pouring out or outpouring of the Spirit gets most of your attention? While further reflecting on it, what other insights emerge for you?

24. "Pentecost Sunday," At the Mass during the Day, Prayer after Communion, 457.

25. "Ritual Masses," V. For the Celebration of Marriage, B, Nuptial Blessing, 1187.

26. Ibid., X. For the Dedication of a Church and an Altar, 2. For the Dedication of An Altar, Collect, 1228.

27. "Masses and Prayers," I. For Holy Church, 9. For Vocations to Holy Orders, Collect, 1256.

28. Ibid., I. For Holy Church, 17. For the Unity of Christians, A, Collect, 1272; "Votive Masses," 10. The Blessed Virgin Mary, B, Our Lady, Mother of the Church, Prayer after Communion, 1349.

29. "Masses and Prayers," I. For Holy Church, 17. For the Unity of Christians, A, Preface, 1274–5.

30. "Votive Masses," 9. The Holy Spirit, A, Prayer after Communion, 1340; B, Collect, 1341.

31. Ibid., 9. The Holy Spirit, B, Prayer after Communion, 1343.

32. "Blessings," 8. The Holy Spirit, 678.

Prayer: Heavenly Father, as you are pleased to nourish my spirit with your enlightening word, so also be pleased to pour the delights of your Holy Spirit into my heart. All glory be yours with your Son, Jesus Christ, and the Holy Spirit forever and ever. Amen.

Spirit Put Upon 1

Scripture: "Here is my servant, whom I uphold, my chosen, in whom my soul delights; I have put my spirit upon him; he will bring forth justice to the nations." (Isa 42:1)

Reflection: Similar to the image associated with pour, pour out, and outpour is that of put upon. In the verse above from the prophet Isaiah, the Spirit is put upon God's servant for the purpose of justice. The verb *to put upon* implies taking advantage of someone for a good purpose; this is exactly what God is doing to the servant he has chosen to put his Spirit upon. In a slightly altered version of the above text, the author of Matthew's Gospel uses it as one of his many fulfillment citations (Matt 12:18); the author of this work employs specific HB (OT) verses, called formula citations, in order to present Jesus as the fulfillment of what Isaiah said. By looking backward, Matthew actually looks forward! Not only is Jesus a part of God's divine plan, according to this author, but Matthew identifies him as the Messiah, the servant of God, upon whom God has put his Spirit.

In Isaiah, the servant declares: "The spirit of the Lord GOD is upon me, because the LORD has anointed me; he has sent me to bring good news to the oppressed, to bind up the brokenhearted, to proclaim liberty to the captives, and release to the prisoners; to proclaim the year of the LORD's favor . . ." (Isa 61:1–2). The servant's mission to others is directed by the Spirit. You may recognize these last two verses of Isaiah as the words the Lukan Jesus reads before delivering his unique inaugural discourse (Luke 4:18–19). The author of Luke's Gospel chose those words to place upon Jesus' lips in the synagogue of Nazareth to serve as a programmatic text, that is, the prophet's words form the Lukan outline for Jesus, God's servant. After reading the words, the Lukan Jesus begins preaching the good news of the kingdom of God to the poor, he heals the blind, and he challenges those who oppress others in any way to release them. He inaugurates the jubilee year of God's favor. Luke, too, understands Jesus to be the fulfillment of God's words presented by the prophet Isaiah; the

Lukan Jesus uniquely states, "Today this scripture has been fulfilled in your hearing" (Luke 4:21). In other words, God takes advantage of Jesus for a good purpose by putting his Spirit upon him.

Journal/Meditation: When have you experienced God putting his Spirit upon you for a good purpose? What was the mission entrusted to you? Did you feel like God was taking advantage of you?

Prayer: Lord GOD, put upon me your Spirit and uphold me in your sight. Make me a messenger of the good news of your Son, Jesus Christ, proclaiming the presence of the kingdom, where he lives and reigns with you and the Holy Spirit, one God, forever and ever Amen.

Spirit Put Upon 2

Scripture: "Balaam looked up and saw Israel camping tribe by tribe. Then the spirit of God came upon him, and he uttered his oracle . . . ." (Num 24:2)

Reflection: Another way to write about the Spirit being put upon someone is found in the verse above from the HB (OT) book of Numbers. Balaam, who has been summoned by Balak to curse (wish evil upon) Israel, ends up blessing Israel because divine inspiration has come upon him. The statement he utters, called an oracle, is the words of God's Spirit. Moses expresses the same idea to Joshua, stating, "Would that all the LORD's people were prophets, and that the LORD would put his spirit on them!" (Num 11:29) The prophet Isaiah presents the LORD giving a mission to Israel (Jacob): ". . . [T]his is my covenant with [Jacob], says the LORD: my spirit that is upon you, and my words that I have put in your mouth, shall not depart out of your mouth, or out of the mouths of your children, or out of the mouths of your children's children, says the LORD, from now on and forever" (Isa 59:21).

The modern word *inspiration* attempts to capture the biblical intent of the Spirit coming upon people or being put on them. The Spirit stimulates the prophet to say what God wants said. Moses' wish is that the LORD would put Spirit on all the people of Israel to encourage them into greater efforts or greater enthusiasm. Isaiah fulfills Moses' wish by emphasizing the permanent nature of God's covenant with Israel through the Spirit that he puts on all the people now, their children, and their grandchildren. Interestingly, the word *inspiration* also refers to breathing, the drawing of air into the lungs. The Hebrew *ruach* (breath, air, wind, spirit) and the Greek *pneuma* (breath, air, wind, spirit) capture all these meanings together. Indeed, God does cause Spirit to come upon us; he does put Spirit upon us.

Journal/Meditation: When have you experienced inspiration? How did that experience involve breath, air, wind, and spirit? How was your course of action changed by the Spirit?

Prayer: LORD God, let your Spirit come upon me that I may be inspired to speak your words. Keep me faithful to the covenant now and forever. Amen.

Filled with Spirit 1

Scripture: "The LORD spoke to Moses: See, I have called by name Bezalel son of Uri son of Hur, of the tribe of Judah: and I have filled him with divine spirit, with ability, intelligence, and knowledge in every kind of craft . . . ." (Exod 31:1–3)

Reflection: After the escape from Egyptian slavery, God tells Moses that with Spirit he has filled Bezalel, a craftsman, to make the tent of meeting, the ark of the covenant, the mercy seat, and all other furnishings (Exod 31:1–11). Later, Moses repeats God's words to the Israelites (Exod 35:30–31; cf. 35:30–35). The metaphor being used here is associated with the verb *to fill*. In order to make a container full, it must first be empty. So, the presumption concerning Bezalel is that he is first without Spirit until the LORD fills him with Spirit. Other aspects of filling include: taking up all or most of the space inside the container; becoming abundantly present and very noticeable; causing someone to feel an emotion powerfully; and electing or appointing someone to hold office and carry out the duties associated with it. All of these aspects can exist simultaneously when Bezalel is filled with Spirit; God fills him with a craftsman's abilities, which make him the obvious choice to make the items required by God, who has already prepared him for this task, which he accepts with abandon (Exod 36:2).

The HB (OT) prophet Micah is very much aware that he, formerly an empty vessel, is filled with the LORD's Spirit. He writes: ". . . [A]s for me, I am filled with power, with the spirit of the LORD, and with justice and might . . ." (Mic 3:8). The OT (A) book written by Jesus son of Sirach (Ecclesiasticus) declares, "When Elijah was enveloped in the whirlwind, Elisha was filled with his spirit" (Sir 48:12a). Elijah's spirit was the Spirit of the LORD, which now filled Elisha (2 Kgs 2:16). As it was for Bezalel, so it was for Elijah and Elisha. The LORD fills his empty prophets, whom he appointed as such, with Spirit, which was abundantly present, very noticeable, and powerfully felt. Before they could be filled they had to be empty; there is only so much room in any container; spirituality includes practices designed to empty ourselves so that the LORD can fill us with Spirit.

Journal/Meditation: What needs to be emptied out of you in order for God to fill you with Spirit? In what specific ways have you experienced being filled with Spirit? What were you called and appointed to do?

Prayer: O LORD, in the past you filled with divine Spirit Bezalel, Micah, Elijah, and Elisha and appointed them to do your will. Fill me with the same Spirit that I may complete the mission you have entrusted to me. I ask this in the name of Jesus, your Son, who lives and reigns with you and the Holy Spirit forever and ever. Amen.

Filled with Spirit 2

Scripture: "... [B]e filled with the Spirit." (Eph 5:18)

Reflection: The section of the Letter to the Ephesians which contains the verse above about being filled with the Spirit begins with the author's notice: "Be careful . . . how you live, not as unwise people but as wise" (Eph 5:15). In other words, spirituality is a way of life lived full of Spirit. The author of Luke's Gospel and the Acts of the Apostles exploits this idea. The first two chapters of Luke's Gospel are uniquely filled with passages about various people being filled with the Spirit in order to prepare for the filling of the apostles with the Spirit on Pentecost. In Luke's Gospel, even before his birth John the Baptist is filled with the Holy Spirit (Luke 1:15), as is Elizabeth, his mother (Luke 1:41), and Zechariah, his father (Luke 1:67). And, of course, Jesus is filled with the Spirit (Luke 4:14). In the Acts of the Apostles, all the apostles are filled with the Holy Spirit (Acts 2:4, 4:31), especially Peter (Acts 4:8), the seven men chosen to wait on tables (Acts 6:3, 5), Stephen (Acts 8:17), Saul (Paul) (Acts 9:17; 13:9), Barnabas (Acts 11:24), and disciples (Acts 13:52).

The metaphor of filling with the Spirit is found in the RM. It occurs in Eucharistic Prayer III where God is asked to fill with his Holy Spirit those who are nourished by the body and blood of Christ.[33] The

---

33. "Order of Mass," par. 113.

Collect for December 20 in Advent refers to the Blessed Virgin Mary as filled with the light of the Holy Spirit;[34] the Collect for St. Barnabas refers to him as being filled with the Holy Spirit;[35] and the Collect for St. Augustine asks God to fill all present with the Spirit,[36] as does that for St. Charles Borromeo.[37] We also ask that the Holy Spirit will fill us with the light of faith.[38] In other words, the author of Ephesians' wish that his readers be filled with the Spirit continues today when we petition God to fill our spirit with his Spirit and live our lives according to his Spirit.

Journal/Meditation: When have you most recently asked God to fill your spirit with his Spirit? How did God answer your prayer?

Prayer: Father, throughout time you have filled the spirit of countless men and women with your Spirit. Fill my spirit with your Holy Spirit that I may live in your light now and enjoy eternal light in your heavenly kingdom, where you are one God—Father, Son, and Holy Spirit—forever and ever. Amen.

Fire of Spirit

Scripture: "Divided tongues, as of fire, appeared among [the apostles], and a tongue rested on each of them." (Acts 2:3)

Reflection: According to the CCC, fire represents "the transforming energy of the Holy Spirit's actions."[39] The Spirit transforms spirit. In the form of divided tongues, as narrated in the Acts of the Apostles above, the Holy Spirit fills the apostles with himself, transforming their spirit into Spirit.[40] Pentecost fulfills God's words in the prophet Isaiah: "... [W]hen you walk through fire you shall not be burned, and the flame shall not consume you" (Isa 43:2b). Both Matthew's Gospel and Luke's Gospel portray John the Baptist announcing that Jesus will baptize with the Holy Spirit and fire (Matt 3:11b; Luke 3:16b). In his First Letter to the Thessalonians, Paul exhorts his readers: "Do not quench the Spirit" (1 Thess 5:19). In other words, do not put out the fire of the Spirit in the

---

34. "Proper of Time," Advent, December 20, Collect, 163.
35. "Proper of Saints," St. Barnabas, June 11, Collect 874.
36. Ibid., St. Augustine, August 28, Collect, 938.
37. Ibid., St. Charles Borromeo, November 4, Collect, 986.
38. "Common of Doctors of the Church," 2, Prayer over the Offerings, 1090.
39. CCC, par. 696.
40. Ibid.

same way that water puts out fire. However, there may be an occasion when the fire needs to be rekindled. The OT (A) First Book of Maccabees records: "The spirit of the people was rekindled when they heard [Simon's] words" (1 Macc 13:7). In other words, Simon, successor to Jonathan and leader of the Jewish army, transforms (fires) the spirit of the people with his inspired words.

The metaphor of fire used for the Spirit is found in the RM and in the OC. In the RM, we ask God to make us aflame with his Spirit.[41] Both the fire of the Spirit and the request that God make us always aflame with that same Spirit are found in the prayer after the second reading of the Pentecost Vigil[42] and in the Prayer after Communion.[43] We ask God to kindle the divine fire of the Holy Spirit in our hearts on January 24, the Memorial of St. Francis de Sales,[44] and on May 20, the Optional Memorial of St. Bernardine of Siena, to be set aflame with the Spirit of God's love.[45] It is the celestial fire of the Spirit with which we ask God to enkindle in our hearts on the Memorial of St. Alphonsus Liguori on August 1,[46] and the fire of the Spirit on the Memorial of St. Bernard on August 20.[47] On September 27, the Memorial of St. Vincent de Paul, our prayer is that God set us afire with the same Spirit that motivated St. Vincent.[48] However, it is in the Solemn Blessing after Confirmation where we acknowledge that the Holy Spirit kindles the fire of charity in the hearts of Jesus' disciples.[49] In a Nuptial Blessing, we ask the Father to use the power of the Spirit to set the newly-married couple's hearts aflame from on high[50] and in the Prayer after Communion after a man or woman makes final religious vows to inflame him or her with the fire of the Holy

---

41. "Proper of Time," Advent, December 17, Prayer after Communion, 160; "Votive Masses," 9. The Holy Spirit, C, Prayer after Communion, 1345.

42. "Pentecost Sunday," At the Vigil Mass, par. 6.

43. Ibid., Simple Form, Prayer after Communion, 452.

44. "Proper of Saints," St. Francis de Sales, January 24, Prayer over the Offerings, 810.

45. Ibid., St. Bernardine of Siena, May 20, Collect, 863.

46. Ibid., St. Alphonsus Liguori, August 1, Prayer over the Offerings, 912.

47. Ibid., St. Bernard, August 20, Collect, 932.

48. Ibid., St. Vincent de Paul, September 27, Collect, 956.

49. "Ritual Masses," I. For the Conferral of the Sacraments of Christian Initiation, 4. For the Conferral of Confirmation, A, Solemn Blessing, 1132; OC, pars. 33, 49.

50. "Ritual Masses," V. For the Celebration of Marriage, C, Nuptial Blessing, 1192.

Spirit.[51] Other fire metaphors employed for the Spirit in the RM include the heavenly fire of the Holy Spirit[52] and, simply, the fire of the Spirit.[53] The OC states that Jesus' ministry was to pour out on the earth the fire of the Spirit.[54] Thus, spirit transformed by Spirit is like being aflame, afire, or set on divine fire.

Journal/Meditation: When has your spirit most recently been transformed by the fire of the Spirit? How would you describe that experience using a fire metaphor?

Prayer: Father, you set on fire your Son's apostles by giving them the Spirit. Send that same Spirit to kindle my spirit that I may share in the ministry of Jesus Christ and continue to feed the flame that set fire on the earth. He lives and reigns with you and the Holy Spirit, one God, forever and ever. Amen.

Spirit Rests On

Scripture: "... [T]he LORD came down in the cloud and spoke to [Moses], and took some of the spirit that was on him and put it on the seventy elders; and when they spirit rested upon them, they prophesied. Two men remained in the camp, ... and the spirit rested on them ...." (Num 11:25a, 26)

Reflection: Other than the account of the Spirit resting on the seventy elders and the two men who remained in the camp—Eldad and Medad (Num 11:26)—the only other person described as having the spirit rest on him is Simeon in Luke's Gospel: "... [T]here was a man in Jerusalem whose name was Simeon; this man was righteous and devout, looking forward to the consolation of Israel, and the Holy Spirit rested on him" (Luke 2:25). In Hebrew, the word for breath, air, wind, or spirit is *ruach*; in Greek, the word for breath, air, wind, or spirit is *pneuma*. The multiple meanings of the word imply that the Spirit moved the seventy-two elders and Simeon to action, just like wind moves whatever it touches; the Spirit settled upon them in the same way that the LORD comes down from heaven in the form of a cloud. The LORD's action fulfills his promise to

---

51. Ibid., VIII. For Religious Profession, 2. For Perpetual Profession, A, Prayer after Communion, 1215.

52. "Masses and Prayers," 39. For Chastity, Collect, 1308.

53. "Votive Masses," 9. The Holy Spirit, C, Prayer over the Offerings, 1344.

54. OC, pars. 22, 39.

Moses: "... I will take some of the spirit that is on you and put it on them; and they shall bear the burden of the people along with you so that you will not bear it all by yourself" (Num 11:17). Simeon receives a revelation from the Spirit and is guided by the Spirit to praise God, according to the narrator in Luke's Gospel (2:26–27). The Spirit cannot be contained; it is like breath, air, and wind. All one can do is cooperate with it.

If we raise our awareness, we might begin to notice that every breath we take is the action of the Spirit resting on—and within—our spirit. All the air that surrounds us is the action of the Spirit encompassing—in which we live and move and have our being—our spirit. Feeling the wind blow through our hair and over our skin is the Spirit resting upon and moving our spirit to action, and it serves as a sensory reminder—like the cloud—of the Spirit's presence. In one of the prophet Zechariah's visions, the four winds or spirits patrol the earth; spirit permeates the universe, but the wind toward the north sets the spirit at rest (Zech 6:5–8). The narrator of John's Gospel says it best: "He whom God has sent speaks the words of God, for he gives the Spirit without measure" (John 3:34). Thus, anyone reviled for the name of Christ, according to the First Letter of Peter, is blessed "because the spirit of glory, which is the Spirit of God, is resting on" him or her (1 Pet 4:14).

Journal/Meditation: How have you experienced the Spirit as breath, air, and wind? To what action did the resting Spirit move your spirit?

Prayer: LORD, your Spirit not only rests upon your people and spurs them to action, but it gives them rest. Without measure settle the Spirit upon my spirit that I may know your will and be moved to carry it out. Hear my prayer in the name of your Son, Jesus Christ, whom you sent to speak your words to me, now and forever. Amen.

Bestowed Spirit

Scripture: "... I think that I too have the Spirit of God." (1 Cor 7:40b)

Reflection: In order to have the Spirit of God, as Paul indicates above in the verse from his First Letter to the Corinthians, the Spirit is bestowed. Earlier in the same letter, the apostle explains that his evangelization of the Corinthians was not with plausible words of wisdom, "but with a demonstration of the Spirit of power" that had been bestowed on him (1 Cor 2:4). In other words, Paul understands himself to be a channel for the Spirit, who powerfully inspires his preached words (1 Thess 1:5;

2:13). According to Paul, we receive "the Spirit that is from God so that we may understand the gifts bestowed on us by God" (1 Cor 2:12), just as Paul attempts to help the Corinthians discern the gifts given by God through the Spirit in his letter to them.

The verb *to bestow* means that someone presents something to somebody. In this reflection, God presents the Spirit to our spirit. The result may be enlightened words or other gifts, as we will see below. In the RM, we are reminded that God first bestowed the Holy Spirit on Pentecost in order to bring to completion the paschal mystery—the suffering, death, resurrection, and ascension of Jesus.[55] God continues to bestow the Spirit when Confirmation is conferred.[56] The OC explains that bishops and priests confer or bestow the Holy Spirit on the baptized.[57] However, because God bestows Spirit, which is like breath, air, and wind, on our spirit, it cannot be captured or contained.

Journal/Meditation: When did God bestow Spirit on your spirit? What were the results?

Prayer: Holy Father, to complete the paschal mystery of your Son, you bestowed the Holy Spirit on his apostles and sent them into the whole world with the good news of your kingdom. Bestow the same Spirit upon my spirit and send me with the gospel of Jesus Christ, who is Lord forever and ever. Amen.

Grace of the Spirit

Scripture: "Grace be with all of you." (Titus 3:15b)

Reflection: The closing of the Letter to Titus does not mention the Spirit directly. As many Bible readers know, letters usually end with some form of greeting that includes the wish that the grace of the Lord Jesus Christ be with the readers (2 Cor 13:13; Gal 6:18; 2 Tim 4:22a; Phil 4:23; 2 Tim 4:22; Phlm 1:25). Like the verse from the Letter to Titus above, Second Timothy also includes this greeting at its end: "Grace be with you" (2 Tim 4:22b). Only the Letter to the Hebrews specifically mentions "the Spirit of grace" (Heb 10:29). According to the CCC, grace is the free

---

55. "Pentecost Sunday," At the Mass during the Day, Preface, 454–456.

56. "Ritual Masses," I. For the Conferral of the Sacraments of Christian Initiation, 4. For the Conferral of Confirmation, A, Inserts for Eucharistic Prayers I, II, II, 1131; OC, par. 58.

57. OC, pars. 22, 39

SPIRIT AS GIFT

and undeserved gift that God gives to people.[58] It is participation in God's very life.[59] In other words, God shares his own divine life with us, and that act of sharing is named grace. The CCC adds that grace is first and above all the gift of the Spirit.[60] The Spirit is given to spirit; divine life is shared with earthly life; people participate in divine life right now. Thus, the wish of grace to someone is the same as wishing him or her the Spirit.

In a Nuptial Blessing for a newly-married couple, God is asked to send down on the man and woman the grace of the Holy Spirit.[61] When seeking forgiveness for sins, we ask God to bestow on us the grace of the Spirit to provoke tears for our offenses.[62] And when praying for our relatives and friends, we acknowledge that by the grace of the Holy Spirit God fills hearts with his gifts of charity.[63] Maybe we don't use the word *grace* or the phrase *the grace of the Spirit*, when we send a birthday card to another—either by way of the post office or the internet—but we are, nevertheless, wishing the grace of the Spirit to the spirit of the person receiving the card. A telephone call may be another way we wish the grace of the Spirit to another. Even behind our "Good morning" greeting may be the wish for the grace of the Spirit to be given to the person we acknowledge. When wishing another the grace of the Spirit and when petitioning God to give the grace of the Spirit for a specific need, we ask God to continue to share his divine life, that is, to continue to infuse the life of the Spirit in others and in ourselves.

Journal/Meditation: In what specific ways have you either directly or indirectly wished others the grace of the Spirit?

Prayer: Send, O God, the grace of the Holy Spirit like a mighty wind into my life that every breath of air I take may be of the divine life you share with your Son, Jesus Christ, in the unity of the Holy Spirit, one God, forever and ever. Amen.

---

58. CCC, par. 1196.
59. Ibid., par. 1997.
60. Ibid., par. 2003.
61. "Ritual Masses," V. For the Celebration of Marriage, A, Nuptial Blessing, 1181.
62. "Masses and Prayers," III. For Various Occasions, 38. For the Forgiveness of Sins, B, Prayer over the Offerings, 1307.
63. Ibid., III. For Various Occasions, 41. For Relatives and Friends, Collect, 1310.

Gentle-Kindly-Patient Spirit

Scripture: "My friends, if anyone is detected in a transgression, you who have received the Spirit should restore such a one in a spirit of gentleness." (Gal 6:1a)

Reflection: In the verse above from Paul's Letter to the Galatians, the apostle expresses his desire that order in the community should be focused on restoration. Those members who have received the Spirit should seek to reincorporate transgressors by touching their spirits with gentleness from Spirit. In his First Letter to the Corinthians he poses the same idea as a question: "What would you prefer? Am I to come to you with a stick, or with love in a spirit of gentleness?" (1 Cor 4:21) We presume that the members of the community in Corinth preferred to be corrected with the Spirit of gentleness. While the patriarchal words concerning a husband's authority over his wife found in the First Letter of Peter need to be critiqued today, the author's basic message to wives about the adornment of their inner selves being "the lasting beauty of a gentle ... spirit, which is very precious in God's sight," should be heeded by both wives and husbands today (1 Pet 3:4). Gentleness flows from the Spirit to spirit.

The OT (A) book of Wisdom declares wisdom—insight, instruction, reflection on the meaning of life, and moral exhortation—to be a kindly spirit, who does not free blasphemers from the guilt of their words, because God's kindly Spirit is connected to their spirit and witnesses their inmost feelings, knows what is in their hearts, and hears the words spoken by their mouths (Wis 1:6). The same idea found in Wisdom is also discovered in a proverb in the HB (OT) book of Ecclesiastes: "Better is the end of a thing than its beginning; the patient in spirit are better than the proud in spirit" (Eccl 7:8). Again, those people who are patient in spirit are calm because the Spirit informs them that the end of something is much better than all the energy required at its beginning. The proud in spirit have no need to be taught by Spirit.

Journal/Meditation: Have you experienced the Spirit connected to your spirit as being gentle, kind, or patient? How? Explain.

Prayer: LORD God, you send your gentle Spirit upon your people to restore them to your presence. Fill me with your kindly Spirit of wisdom and instruct me with your patient Spirit that I may know how much better is the end of my life in your service than its beginning. Hear this prayer in the name of your Son, Jesus Christ, who is Lord forever and ever. Amen.

Good-Quiet-Noble Spirit

Scripture: "Teach me to do your will, for you are my God. Let your good spirit lead me on a level path." (Ps 143:10)

Reflection: In Psalm 143, the singer asks God to lead him on a level path with his good Spirit. In this prayer for help, the psalmist acknowledges that his future depends on the Spirit. Similarly, in a lengthy prayer, Ezra the priest recounts how God gave his "good spirit" to instruct the Israelites in the wilderness (Neh 9:20); their future depended upon God feeding them and giving them water. Likewise, in their letter to Gentile believers, the apostles and elders state, ". . . [I]t has seemed good to the Holy Spirit and to us to impose on you no further burden than these essentials" (Acts 15:28): abstain from meat sacrificed to idols, blood, what is strangled, and fornication (Acts 15:29). The future of Gentile believers depends on their adherence to the terms of the letter sent to them.

The patriarchal words concerning a husband's authority over his wife in the First Letter of Peter need to be critiqued today, but the author's basic message to wives about the adornment of their inner selves being "the lasting beauty of a . . . quiet spirit, which is very precious in God's sight," should be heeded by both wives and husbands today (1 Pet 3:4). Quietness flows from the Spirit to spirit and engenders a future of marital happiness. The mother, who watched her seven sons perish in a single day, is described by the narrator of the Second Book of Maccabees as being "[f]illed with a noble spirit" (2 Macc 7:21b). She encouraged each son with her highest ideals to entrust his future into the hands of his Creator instead of obeying the king. The future of this life, as well as the future of life hereafter, depends on the good, quiet, and noble Spirit connecting to spirit.

Journal/Meditation: Have you experienced the Spirit connected to your spirit as being good, quiet, or noble? How? Explain.

Prayer: O LORD, you saved your people in the wilderness by giving them food, water, and good Spirit to instruct them. Teach me, like you taught them, to do your will. Grant that your good, quiet, and noble Spirit will lead me on a level path in this life to the eternal one in your kingdom, where you are one God—Father, Son, and Holy Spirit—forever and ever. Amen.

Dauntless Spirit

Scripture: "By his dauntless spirit [Isaiah] saw the future, and comforted the mourners in Zion." (Sir 48:24)

Reflection: Jesus son of Sirach praises the dauntless Spirit of the prophet Isaiah for the comfort he showed to Zion (Isa 40:1; 51:3; 61:2; 66:13). The prophet was unable to be frightened or discouraged by the fall of Judah and Jerusalem to the Babylonians in 586 BCE; he trusted that God would bring back the captives. Like the author of the HB (OT) book of Proverbs, he knew that the human spirit can endure many things—another way to declare it dauntless—but people cannot bear a broken spirit (Prov 18:14). In the book of the prophet Daniel, Daniel is described as "a man . . . who is endowed with a spirit of the holy gods, . . . [who] was found to have enlightenment, understanding, and wisdom like the wisdom of the gods" (Dan 4: 8–9, 18; 5:11). " . . . [A]n excellent spirit, knowledge, and understanding to interpret dreams, explain riddles, and solve problems were found in . . . Daniel . . ." (5:12a). Later in the same book, it is confirmed that an excellent Spirit—that made him dauntless—is found in Daniel (Dan 6:3).

An endowed, dauntless Spirit can astonish us (2 Macc 7:12). That is why we ask God to endow us with the Spirit of his Son,[64] to renew in the church the Spirit with which he endowed St. Augustine,[65] to instruct those who have been endowed with the gifts of the Holy Spirit,[66] and to endow with the Spirit of wisdom those to whom God has handed authority to govern: bishops.[67] In all these requests, we ask the Father to provide people with the Spirit, who gives them desirable qualities, abilities, and characteristics. When Spirit connects to spirit, we become filled with a dauntless Spirit.

---

64. "Appendix," Eucharistic Prayer for Reconciliation II, par. 7; "Appendices," Appendix IV, Rite of Blessing a Chalice and a Paten within Mass, par. 7.

65. "Proper of Saints," St. Augustine, August 28, Collect, 938.

66. "Ritual Masses," I. For the Conferral of the Sacraments of Christian Initiation, 4. For the Conferral of Confirmation, B, Prayer after Communion, 1134.

67. Ibid., IV. For the Conferral of Holy Orders, 1. For the Ordination of a Bishop, A, Solemn Blessing, 1144; B, Solemn Blessing, 1150.

Journal/Meditation: When has the Spirit made your spirit dauntless? What was the occasion? What quality, ability, and characteristic emerged from you?

Prayer: O God, you endowed your prophets Isaiah and Daniel with your own excellent, divine Spirit to enlighten them with understanding and wisdom. Endow my spirit with your Spirit that I may be dauntless all the days of my life. Hear me through Jesus Christ, your Son, now and forever. Amen.

Fruits of Spirit

Scripture: "... [W]e ourselves, who have the first fruits of the Spirit groan inwardly while we wait for adoption, the redemption of our bodies." (Rom 8:23)

Reflection: In Jewish understanding, the beginning of a harvest was called the first fruits. Whatever was first harvested of grain, grapes, olives, etc. is considered sacred and belonging to God. Thus, when Paul writes to the Romans, he identifies those in whom the Spirit of God dwells (Rom 8:9) as possessing the first fruits of the Spirit with more to come. In his letter to the Galatians, he lists the fruits of the Spirit: "... love, joy, peace, patience, kindness, generosity, faithfulness, gentleness, and self-control" (Gal 5:22–23). The CCC explains, "The fruits of the Spirit are perfections that the Holy Spirit forms in us as the first fruits of eternal glory."[68] Then, the CCC lists the twelve traditional fruits: "charity, joy, peace, patience, kindness, goodness, generosity, gentleness, faithfulness, modesty, self-control, chastity."[69] In his First Letter to the Corinthians, Paul lists what he calls spiritual gifts, which can be considered to be first fruits of the Spirit also. The apostle writes:

> Now there are varieties of gifts, but the same Spirit.... To each is given the manifestation of the Spirit for the common good. To one is given through the Spirit the utterance of wisdom, and to another the utterance of knowledge according to the same Spirit, to another faith by the same Spirit, to another gifts of healing by the one Spirit, to another the working of miracles, to another prophecy, to another the discernment of spirits, to another various kinds of tongues, to another the interpretation of tongues. All these are activated by one and the same Spirit,

---

68. CCC, par. 1832.
69. Ibid.

who allots to each one individually just as the Spirit chooses." (1 Cor 12:4, 7–11)

One other fruit of the Spirit is freedom. In Paul's Second Letter to the Corinthians, he declares that "where the Spirit of the Lord is, there is freedom" (2 Cor 3:17). This fruit—freedom—means that we are no longer bound by the three-hundred thirteen precepts of Torah; in other words, we no longer have to earn salvation. The Spirit brings about freedom from the Law (Rom 8:14–16). No matter what the fruits of the Spirit may be, their common source is the Spirit, and their intended purpose is the common good, the good of the whole community.

While there is minimal reference to the fruits of the Spirit in the RM, there are, nevertheless, a few citations. For instance, we declare that we have received the first fruits of the Spirit and hope for an everlasting share of them.[70] Eucharistic Prayer IV and the Pentecost Vigil identify the Spirit as the first fruits sent to those who believe.[71] God is asked to nurture carefully the fruits of the Spirit[72] in us that we may carry out in freedom of Spirit what pleases him.[73] Then, according to the OC, we will be able to express our faith by means of the fruits the Spirit has produced in us.[74] The manifestation of the fruits of the Spirit in our lives remind us that when Spirit connects to spirit, there flows all types of charity, joy, peace, patience, kindness, goodness, generosity, gentleness, faithfulness, modesty, self-control, chastity, wisdom, knowledge, faith, healing miracles, prophecy, discernment, tongues, interpretation, freedom, and more. Their common source is the Spirit, who gives them to spirit to be used for the common good.

Journal/Meditation: What fruits of the Spirit have you received? How have you used them for the common good?

Prayer: Eternal God, you have given your people the first fruits of the Spirit. Nurture carefully the fruits you have bestowed upon me that in freedom I may do what pleases you and express my faith in your Son, Jesus Christ, who with you and the Holy Spirit are one God forever and ever. Amen.

---

70. "Order of Mass," par. 57.
71. Ibid., par. 117; "Pentecost Sunday," At the Vigil Mass, Extended Form, par. 3.
72. "Masses and Prayers," 27. At Seedtime, A, Prayer over the Offerings, 1292.
73. "Proper of Saints," St. Raymond of Penyafort, January 7, Collect, 806.
74. OC, par. 4.

3

Spirit Speaks

Spirit of Father Speaks

Scripture: Jesus said to his disciples, "When [Jewish and Gentile judges] bring you to trial and hand you over, do not worry beforehand about what you are to say; but say whatever is given you at that time, for it is not you who speak, but the Holy Spirit." (Mark 13:11)

Reflection: While most early Christians—both Jewish and Gentile—would have been terrified at the thought of having to defend themselves in some kind of a public trial, the Markan Jesus removes their anxiety by telling them that the Spirit will provide their proper defense. Patience is required while they await the words of the Spirit coming from their spirit-speaking lips. The author of Matthew's Gospel copies the same verse from Mark but adds that it is "the Spirit of your Father speaking through you" (Matt 10:20). In a similar vein, while addressing the issue of prophecy, the author the Second Letter of Peter reminds his readers that "no prophecy ever came by human will, but men and women moved by the Holy Spirit spoke from God" (2 Pet 1:21). Likewise, the author of the First Letter to Timothy declares, "Now the Spirit expressly says that in later times some will renounce the faith by paying attention to deceitful spirits and teachings of demons" (1 Tim 4:1). The Letter to the Hebrews identifies words of the Spirit (Heb 3:7) contained in Psalm 95:7b–11.

Luke's Acts of the Apostles records the Holy Spirit saying, "Set apart for me Barnabas and Saul for the work to which I have called them" (Acts 13:2). The CB (NT) book of Revelation captures many of the exact words of the Spirit. John of Patmos records: "... I heard a voice from heaven saying, 'Write this: Blessed are the dead who from now on die in the Lord.' 'Yes,' says the Spirit, 'they will rest from their labors, for their deeds follow them'" (Rev 14:13). Later, the author states, "... [T]he testimony of Jesus is the spirit of prophecy" (Rev 19:10), and "The Spirit and the bride say, 'Come'" (Rev 22:17a). Earlier in Revelation, the Son of Man, who dictates seven letters for John to write and send to seven churches, includes this line in every letter: "Let anyone who has an ear listen to what the Spirit is saying to the churches" (Rev 2:7a, 11a, 17a, 29; 3:6, 13, 22). In other words, the words of the Spirit are in the words of the letters addressed to the members of the churches; if they listen to the words, they are listening to the Spirit. Spirit connects to spirit through words written on a page, through disciples, and directly to others.

Journal/Meditation: What has the Spirit said to your spirit through written words, through other disciples of Jesus, or directly to you?

Prayer: Father of Jesus, your Spirit speaks through your Son's followers. Increase your grace in me that I may listen to what the Spirit says to me and not fear to speak the Spirit's words. Hear my spiritual prayer through the same Holy Spirit now and forever. Amen.

Spirit Reveals

Scripture: "In former generations this mystery was not made known to humankind, as it has now been revealed to [Christ's] holy apostles and prophets by the Spirit: that is, the Gentiles have become fellow heirs, members of the same body, and sharers in the promise in Christ Jesus through the gospel." (Eph 3:5–6)

Reflection: Another way the Spirit speaks to spirit is through revelation. In the Letter to the Ephesians, the author declares that the Spirit has revealed that Jews and Gentiles are members of the same body. In the religious world of the first century CE, this is quite a revelation to Jews, because they considers themselves to be God's chosen people alone, and the Gentiles, whom the Jews thought were unclean, considered Judaism to be a very odd religion. Now, by revelation of the Spirit, Jews and Gentiles are united through the preaching of the gospel. The Gospel of Luke's unique character named Simeon is declared to be an instrument of the Spirit three times (Luke 2:25–27). However, the second time states, "It had been revealed to him by the Holy Spirit that he would not see death before he had seen the Lord's Messiah" (Luke 2:26). Like the author of the Letter to the Ephesians, the author of Luke's Gospel considers one role of the Spirit to be the revelation of truth. The Spirit communicates to Simeon's spirit that he would not die until he had gazed upon the Lord's anointed one, Jesus.

The Prayer over the Offerings for the Mass during Pentecost Day asks God that the Holy Spirit reveals more abundantly the hidden mystery of the sacrifice of Jesus Christ under the forms of bread and wine and that he lead the worshipers into all truth.[1] Likewise, in the preface for Pentecost we are reminded that it was the Spirit who opened to all people the knowledge of God, that is, revealed God to the Gentiles.[2] The Preface for the Feast of the Presentation of the Lord refers to the passage from Luke's Gospel above about Simeon when it states that the Spirit revealed Jesus to be the glory of Israel and the light of the nations.[3] If revelation is defined as surprising and valuable information that is newly disclosed—maybe even formerly hidden—then the Spirit is busy revealing to spirit truths that humankind could not discover alone.

Journal/Meditation: What revelation have you received from the Spirit? Was it surprising, valuable, formerly hidden? Explain what you did with the truth revealed to you by the Spirit?

Prayer: Holy Spirit, you revealed Jesus to be the glory of the Jews and the light of the Gentiles. Reveal to my spirit the presence of the Father, who with you and Jesus Christ are one God forever and ever. Amen.

Spirit Testifies

Scripture: ". . . [T]he Spirit is the one that testifies, for the Spirit is the truth. There are three that testify: the Spirit and the water and the blood, these three agree." (1 John 5:6b–7)

Reflection: The verb *to testify* means to make a factual statement based on personal experience or to declare something to be true from

---

1. "Pentecost Sunday," At the Mass during the Day, Prayer over the Offerings, 453.
2. Ibid., Preface, 454–456.
3. "Proper of Saints," The Presentation of the Lord, February 2, At the Mass, Preface, 820–821.

personal experience. This is the role of the Spirit according to the author of the First Letter of John. To what is the Spirit testifying? John answers that it is to the belief that Jesus is the anointed one (Messiah, Christ). And if the Spirit's testimony is not enough, according to First John, the water and blood that flowed from Jesus' side on the cross serve as two more testifiers (John 19:34–35). The Johannine Jesus makes the Spirit's role very clear when he states that the Spirit who comes from the Father will testify on his behalf (John 15:26). Likewise, the author of the Letter to the Hebrews considers the Holy Spirit testifying through the words of the prophet Jeremiah (Heb 10:15; Jer 31:33).

In his Letter to the Romans, Paul writes, "I am speaking the truth in Christ—I am not lying; my conscience confirms it by the Holy Spirit" (Rom 9:1). In effect, to have one's conscience confirm the truth is the activity of Spirit connected to spirit. This leads the apostle to declare "that no one speaking by the Spirit of God ever says 'Let Jesus be cursed!' and no one can say 'Jesus is Lord' except by the Holy Spirit" (1 Cor 12:3). Later, in his First Letter to the Corinthians he applies the same idea to speaking in tongues: "For those who speak in a tongue do not speak to other people but to God; for nobody understands them, since they are speaking mysteries in the Spirit" (1 Cor 14:2). The OC states that speaking in tongues is usually no longer a manifestation of the Spirit,[4] but Paul's point remains: When Spirit is connected to spirit, falsity cannot be uttered because one's conscious will not permit it. Tongues, a manifestation of Spirit, are a form of prayer that moves from God's Spirit to human spirit and back to God again. In other words, this form of prayer finds Spirit serving as the mediator between God and spirit. Thus, the individual can testify on personal prayer experience to the truth that Spirit speaks through spirit.

Journal/Meditation: To what truth has the Spirit inspired you to testify?

Prayer: All holy God, your Spirit, who is truth, testifies to the lordship of your Son, Jesus Christ. Open my ears to hear the Spirit speaking in your Scriptures, in my friends, and in my own words. Grant this prayer in the name of Jesus now and forever. Amen.

---

4. OC, pars. 22, 39.

Spirit Captive

Scripture: Paul said to the elders of the church in Ephesus: ". . . [A]s a captive to the Spirit, I am on my way to Jerusalem, not knowing what will happen to me there, except that the Holy Spirit testifies to me in every city that imprisonment and persecutions are waiting for me." (Acts 20:22–23)

Reflection: The author of the Acts of the Apostles—the same person who wrote Luke's Gospel—presents Paul addressing the leaders of the church in Ephesus. He tells them that he is bound in the spirit. Being a captive implies that he is a prisoner of the Spirit, minimally enslaved by the Spirit and unable to escape from what the Spirit has planned for him: imprisonment and persecutions. After a stop in Tyre, where "[t]hrough the Spirit [disciples] told Paul not to go on to Jerusalem" (Acts 21:4), he went on to Caesarea, where "a prophet named Agabus came . . . and took Paul's belt, bound his own feet and hands with it, and said, 'Thus says the Holy Spirit, "This is the way the Jews in Jerusalem will bind the man who owns this belt and will hand him over to the Gentiles"'" (Acts 21:10–11). The author of Acts can portray Paul, disciples, and Agabus predicting all that will happen to the apostle because in the rest of the book he will narrate how Paul got to Jerusalem, his arrest, his acknowledgment of being a Roman citizen, his appeal to Felix the governor, his imprisonment, his appeal to Porcius Festus the governor who succeeded Felix, his appeal to the emperor, and his trip to Rome (Acts 21:1—28:31). According to Luke, all this occurs because Paul is a captive to the Spirit.

At first, this concept of being a prisoner of the Spirit may revolt all of us free-loving United States citizens. However, maybe Paul was like the psalmist: "I commune with my heart in the night; I meditate and search my spirit" (Ps 77:6). Maybe, like Jonathan in the First Book of Maccabees, "his spirit was aroused" (1 Macc 10:74), or like Jesus he trusted that he would be "vindicated in spirit" (1 Tim 3:16). As a captive to the Spirit, "the sword of the Spirit, which is the word of God" (Eph 6:17), for Paul was "living and active, sharper than any two-edged sword, piercing until it divides soul from spirit, . . . able to judge the thoughts and intentions of the heart" (Heb 4:12). Not only did God know what was in Paul's heart, God was the source for what was there. God's Spirit spoke frequently to Paul's spirit, and Paul listened to what the Spirit was saying to him.

Journal/Meditation: In what specific ways is your spirit captive to the Spirit? What has the Spirit said to your spirit?

Prayer: Father, you made Paul a captive to your Spirit so that the gospel of your Son, Jesus Christ, was preached to the nations of the world. Send that same Spirit to me that your living and active word may judge the thoughts and reflections of my spirit and bind me closer to you now and forever. Amen.

Spirit Comes Upon

Scripture: "The spirit of the LORD came upon [Othniel], and he judged Israel . . . ." (Judg 3:10)

Reflection: There are a number of biblical characters upon whom the Spirit comes. The spirit of the LORD is understood to be the force that empowers chosen individuals to perform extraordinary deeds of leadership and strength. In other words, the Spirit connects to their spirit. The first of these people to have the Spirit come upon him is Othniel, who gets only a three-verse mention in the HB (OT) book of Judges (3:9–11). The next person upon whom the Spirit comes is Jephthah (Judg 11:29), who has a back story with several chapters devoted to his exploits (Judg 10:6—12:7). The spirit of God comes upon King Saul (1 Sam 11:6) and upon his messengers (1 Sam 19:20), upon Amasai (1 Chr 12:18), Azariah (2 Chr 15:1), and Jahaziel (2 Chr 20:14).

Othniel and Jephthah are empowered by the Spirit to lead Israel's army into war and conquer the enemies. Saul is empowered to be king. Amasai presents men to David, who makes them officers of his troops. Azariah is empowered to empower others to act on God's behalf. And Jahaziel is empowered with the Spirit to deliver a message to King Jehoshaphat that God will defeat their enemies because the upcoming battle belongs to him. Worthy of reflection, and next in line, is you, the reader. If the Spirit of God came upon people of the past, the Spirit must still come upon people today. If we keep in mind that the Spirit of the LORD is the force that empowers us to perform extraordinary deeds of leadership and strength, we might discover in retrospect that the Spirit did, indeed, come upon our spirit and speak in and through our words and deeds.

Journal/Meditation: When have you experienced the Spirit coming upon you and empowering you to perform an extraordinary deed of leadership and strength?

Prayer: All-holy Father, let your Spirit come upon me that I may be empowered to leadership in faith. Grant me the strength to bear witness to Jesus Christ, your Son, who with you and the Holy Spirit are one God forever and ever. Amen.

Spirit Takes Possession

Scripture: "... [T]he spirit of the LORD took possession of Gideon...." (Judg 6:34)

Reflection: When the Spirit takes possession of someone, as in the case of Gideon above, the Spirit assumes control of his spirit. Once Spirit takes possession of spirit, the LORD begins to rescue his people from their enemies. The narrative about Gideon's exploits under the Spirit's control occupies Judges 6:11 through 8:35. After Samuel has anointed Saul as the first king of Israel, he tells him that the spirit of the LORD will possess him when he meets a band of prophets and so it happens (1 Sam 10:6, 10). After Samuel anoints David king of Israel, the spirit of the LORD departs from Saul because God has rejected him (1 Sam 16:14). The Second Book of Chronicles notes that "the spirit of God took possession of Zechariah son of the priest Jehoida" (2 Chr 24:20); the Spirit connects to Zechariah's spirit and he reminds the Israelites that they have transgressed the LORD's commandments. However, the king does not like hearing Zechariah's words and orders him stoned to death.

The interesting common denominator in these biblical accounts of the Spirit taking possession of spirit is the rescue of God's people. Once the Spirit takes possession of Gideon, he proceeds to rescue Israel from the Midianites. Once the Spirit takes possession of Saul, he defeats the Ammonites, Philistines, and Amalekites. Once the Spirit takes possession of the prophet Zechariah, he reminds the people of Israel that they need to turn from their idolatry and re-embrace the LORD's commandments. In other words, he attempts to rescue the people, but they conspire against him, and King Joash (Jehoash) (835–796 BCE) orders him stoned to death in the temple court. Sometimes people refuse to hear the inspired words of God's prophet. According to the Creed in the RM, the Spirit speaks through the prophets.[5]

Journal/Meditation: Has the Spirit ever taken possession of you? Whom did you rescue? What words were you inspired to speak?

---

5. "Order of Mass," par 18.

Prayer: O LORD, when you Spirit took possession of Gideon, Saul, and Zechariah, you rescued your people. Let your Spirit take possession of the leaders of churches and countries that your words may be spoken and your will be made known today, tomorrow, and forever. Amen.

Spirit Stirred 1

Scripture: "The spirit of the LORD began to stir [Samson] . . . ." (Judg 13:25)

Reflection: In the biblical world, the spirit can come upon, take possession of, or stir a person to action. Such is the case with Samson, who may be one of the more famous judges of Israel. His story begins with a narrative that resembles the one about the barrenness of Sarah, wife of Abraham. Samson's parents, Manoah and his unnamed, barren wife, conceive a son, whose spirit is stirred by Spirit. From Judges 13:2 through 16:31, the reader is told that the spirit of the LORD rushes on him, enabling him to kill a lion (Judg 14:6), to kill his people's enemy (Judg 14:19), and to give him strength to break the ropes that bind him and kill a thousand men (Judg 15:14). But Samson is not the only person the Spirit stirs.

The narrator of the Second Book of Chronicles ends his work by writing, ". . . [T]he LORD stirred up the spirit of King Cyrus of Persia so that he sent a herald throughout all his kingdom and also declare in a written edict: 'Thus says King Cyrus of Persia: The LORD, the God of heaven, has given me all the kingdoms of the earth, and he has charged me to build him a house at Jerusalem, which is in Judah. Whoever is among you of all his people, may the LORD his God be with him! Let him go up'" (2 Chr 36:22–23). The same words are repeated at the beginning of the HB (OT) book of Ezra (1:1–3). Those words carry little to none of the shock they caused in the mind of the authors of those two books. Cyrus is a Gentile; he is not a Jew. The prophet Isaiah even calls him the LORD's anointed (Isa 45:1). The Spirit is sent to Cyrus's spirit to stir him to defeat Babylon, the place of Jewish captivity, and, thus, enable the Jewish survivors to return to their homeland. The Gentile Cyrus declares that the Jewish God has given him the whole world, stirred him to rebuild Jerusalem's Temple, and inspired him to release the Jewish captives he found in Babylon so they can return to Jerusalem. The LORD's Spirit can stir an Israelite Samson, a Gentile Cyrus, and you, the reader. The Spirit cannot be contained! The idea that just now inspired you is the Spirit stirring your spirit.

Journal/Meditation: What has the Spirit stirred in your spirit? Explain.

Prayer: In times past, Father, your Spirit stirred the spirit of Samson and the spirit of Cyrus. Stir my spirit with your Spirit that I may embrace your will and carry it out in the name of your Son, Jesus the Anointed One, who with you and the Holy Spirit are one God forever and ever Amen.

Spirit Stirred 2

Scripture: "The heads of the families of Judah and Benjamin, and the priests and the Levites—everyone whose spirit God had stirred—got ready to go up and rebuild the house of the LORD in Jerusalem." (Ezra 1:5).

Reflection: The biblical story of the return to Jerusalem of the Jewish exiles in Babylon begins with the record of the LORD's words in the prophet Jeremiah: "I am going to stir up a destructive wind against Babylon and against the inhabitants of Lebqamai; and I will send winnowers to Babylon, and they shall winnow her" (Jer 51:1–2a). God states that he will stir up the spirit of a destroyer—who becomes Cyrus of Persia—who will overcome Babylon (Chaldea and Lebqamai are other names for Babylon)—and winnow—that is, remove undesirable parts, like one separates grain from husks (chaff)—her. Once this is accomplished, some of the spirits of the Jews are stirred by the Spirit to return to Jerusalem, where they will rebuild the Temple. The prophet Haggai states, ". . . [T]he LORD stirred up the spirit of Zerubbabel son of Shealtiel, governor of Judah, and the spirit of Joshua son of Jehozadak, the high priest, and the spirit of all the remnant of the people; and they came and worked on the house of the LORD of hosts, their God" (Hag 1:14). In the RM, we ask the Lord to stir up the Spirit in the church that filled St. Josaphat to lay down his life for his people and to strengthen us by the same Spirit to be willing to do the same.[6]

At an earlier time in Israelite history, "the God of Israel stirred up the spirit of King Pul of Assyria, the spirit of King Tilgath-pilneser of Assyria, and he carried them away, namely, the Reubenites, the Gadites, and

---

6. "Proper of Saints," St. Josaphat, November 12, Collect, 993.

the half-tribe of Manasseh, and brought them to Halah, Habor, Hara, and the river Gozan, to this day" (1 Chr 5:26). For the chronicler, idolatry is the reason God stirred up the spirit of his people's enemies (1 Chr 5:25). From a biblical perspective—one which we may not like today—God can stir up the spirit of Assyria, the enemy of his people living in the Transjordan, in order to punish their infidelity with exile. Thus, the LORD may stir spirit with Spirit for good, or he may stir spirit with Spirit to punish.

Journal/Meditation: When have you experience your spirit being stirred by Spirit? Did the stirring prompt you to do good, or did it prompt some type of punishment?

Prayer: Come, Holy Spirit, like a mighty wind, and stir my spirit to do the Father's will. I ask this in the name of Jesus, who with you and the Father are one God forever and ever. Amen.

Spirit Guide

Scripture: ". . . [S]ome of those who belonged to the synagogue of the Freedmen . . . stood up and argued with Stephen. But they could not withstand the wisdom and the Spirit with which he spoke." (Acts 6:9–10)

Reflection: One of the underlying themes of Luke's Acts of the Apostles is the guidance of the Spirit. Once Pentecost occurs in the Acts, the author portrays the Spirit directing the activity of Jesus' disciples and those they choose to help them. For example, there is Stephen, who is described as full of the Spirit and of wisdom (Acts 6:3), chosen to be one of seven men to serve the poor. As the above verses make clear, Stephen's opponents could not withstand the Spirit and wisdom with which he spoke. Another of the seven is Philip to whom the Spirit speaks: "Go over to this chariot and join it" (Acts 8:29). After instructing the Ethiopian eunuch in the chariot and baptizing him, the Spirit of the Lord snatches Philip away to proclaim the good news elsewhere (Acts 8:39).

After Peter has a vision and is thinking about it, the Spirit says to him, "Look, three men are searching for you. Now get up, go down, and go with them without hesitation; for I have sent them" (Acts 10:19–20). Peter goes with the three men and launches the mission to the Gentiles in Joppa. Later, Peter narrates to the rest of the apostles in Jerusalem how the Spirit told him to go with the three men and not to make a distinction between Jews and Gentiles (Acts 11:12). The author of the Acts also mentions a prophet named Agabus from Jerusalem who went to Antioch and "stood up and predicted by the Spirit that there would be a severe famine over all the world; and this took place during the reign of Claudius" (Acts 11:28). The famine sparks a relief mission by Barnabas and Saul, both of whom are full of the Holy Spirit (Acts 11:24; 9:17). Later in the Acts, the author writes: "[T]he Holy Spirit said, 'Set apart for me Barnabas and Saul for the work to which I have called them'" (Acts 13:2); the author concludes that they were "sent out by the Holy Spirit" (Acts 13:4). Thus does the author of the Acts of the Apostles present the Spirit directing the activity of Jesus' apostles and those they choose to help them. The OC exhorts those about to be confirmed to be living members of the church under the guidance of the Spirit.[7]

Journal/Meditation: In what specific experience of your life have you experienced the guidance of the Spirit? Were you filled with wisdom and/or some ability to predict something? Did the Spirit speak to you?

Prayer: Father, your wisdom and Spirit were manifest in your servants Stephen, Philip, Peter, and Agabus. Just as you guided their activity, so guide my spirit today, tomorrow, and forever. Hear my prayer through Jesus Christ my Lord. Amen.

---

7. OC, pars. 23, 39.

4

Powerful Spirit

Power of the Spirit 1

Scripture: "May the God of hope fill you with all joy and peace in believing, so that you may abound in hope by the power of the Holy Spirit." (Rom 15:13)

Reflection: In Paul's one-verse prayer above, found in his Letter to the Romans, the apostle wishes his readers hope that comes from the power of the Spirit. He began the letter stating that "[Jesus] was declared to be Son of God with power according to the spirit of holiness by resurrection from the dead . . ." (Rom 1:4). And he names the power of the Spirit of God as one of the ways he has enabled Gentiles to believe in the gospel (Rom 15:19). In his First Letter to the Thessalonians, he writes that the message of the gospel came to the Thessalonians "not in word only but also in power and in the Holy Spirit and with full conviction" (1 Thess 1:5). In other words, Paul attributes the Spirit with holiness, the strength to raise Jesus from the dead, the ability to give hope, and the capacity to convince Gentiles of the truth of the gospel. This is what Paul means by the power of the Spirit.

In the RM, it is the power of the Holy Spirit that enables various individuals to be gathered into the body of Christ through their sharing of the body and blood of Christ.[1] The power of the Spirit fills the members

---

1. "Appendix," Eucharistic Prayers for Reconciliation, I, par. 7.

with life, and the power of the Spirit of love enables them to be counted among the members of Christ's body.[2] As pilgrims in this world, the power of the Spirit leads people to the Father's kingdom.[3] It is the power of the Spirit that the Father uses to gather people, scattered by sin, to himself[4] after giving life to all things and making them holy by the power of the Spirit.[5] The OC declares that the already-baptized receive the power of the Spirit when they are confirmed.[6] In a time when the word *power* may carry the baggage of negativity, the power of the Spirit carries the baggage of holiness, strength, hope, truth, unity, life, and leadership to the eternal kingdom.

Journal/Meditation: In what specific way(s) have you experienced the power of the Spirit?

Prayer: O LORD, by the power of the Spirit you give life to everything and make everything holy. Hear my prayer of thanksgiving for your gift and inspire me to see such powerful presence throughout your universe. I ask this in the name of Jesus, your Son, now and forever. Amen.

Power of the Spirit 2

Scripture: The risen Jesus said to his apostles: ". . . [Y]ou will receive power when the Holy Spirit has come upon you; and you will be my witnesses in Jerusalem, in all Judea and Samaria, and to the ends of the earth." (Acts 1:8)

Reflection: In the Acts of the Apostles, the second volume of Luke's Gospel, the narrator states that the risen Jesus gave instructions through the Holy Spirit to his apostles (Acts 1:2) and told them that they would receive the power of the Holy Spirit to be witnesses in Jerusalem, Judea, Samaria, and to the ends of the earth. The power of the Spirit is received by the apostles on Pentecost. The power of the Spirit establishes the geographical outline for the rest of the book, which ends with Paul in Rome. The author of the Second Letter of Timothy reminds his readers that God did not give them "a spirit of cowardice, but rather a spirit of power" (2

---

2. Ibid., Eucharistic Prayer for Use in Masses for Various Needs I, pars. 1, 7; II, par. 7; III, par. 7; IV, par. 7.

3. Ibid., II, par. 1.

4. "Order of Mass," par. 59.

5. Ibid., par. 108.

6. OC, pars. 22, 39.

Tim 1:7). And the prayer voiced by the author of the Letter to the Ephesians asks God to grant his readers strength in their inner being "with power through his Spirit" (Eph 3:16). Thus, the Spirit enables otherwise fearful people's spirit with the capacity to declare Jesus raised from the dead when reason dictates that to be impossible. The inner being or spirit is empowered by Spirit with the necessary strength to live one's life connected to the divine presence.

In the RM, the Lord is asked to send the power of the Spirit into the fullness of the water of the baptismal font so that those baptized in it will be reborn in the Spirit.[7] We pray that the power of the Spirit come to us,[8] that it overshadow us in the same way as it did the Blessed Virgin Mary,[9] and that it make us docile in believing the faith and courageous in confessing it.[10] We ask the Father to set the hearts of a newly-married couple aflame with the power of the Spirit,[11] and, on the anniversary of religious profession, we ask the Father to conform the jubilarian more fully to the image of Jesus by the power of the Spirit.[12] We also ask that the power of the Spirit remove divisions between Christians[13] because by the power of the Spirit God comes unfailing to our aid.[14] All of these requests for the power of the Spirit to connect to our spirit are petitions for divine strength to live our lives in witness to the resurrection of Christ.

Journal/Meditation: What power of the Spirit do you need today?

Prayer: I know that you come unfailingly to my aid, Holy Father, with the power of the Holy Spirit. Overshadow me with the Spirit today that I may be an instrument of unity among people and a witness to the resurrection of Jesus Christ, your Son, who lives and reigns with you and the Holy Spirit, one God, forever and ever. Amen.

---

7. "Easter Sunday," pars. 44, 46.

8. "Proper of Time," Easter Time, 439.

9. "Proper of Saints," Annunciation of the Lord, March 25, Preface, 842–843.

10. Ibid., St. Sixtus II, August 7, Collect, 920; "Common of Martyrs," II. During Easter Time, A. For Several Martyrs, Collect, 1062.

11. "Ritual Masses," V. For the Celebration of Marriage, C, Nuptial Blessing, 1192.

12. "Masses and Prayers," I. For Holy Church, 13. For Religious, B, Prayer over the Offerings, 1265.

13. Ibid., 17. For the Unity of Christians, C, Collect, 1278.

14. "Votive Masses," 9. The Holy Spirit, B, Preface, 1342–1343.

Laying on of Hands

Scripture: "... [T]he LORD said to Moses, 'Take Joshua son of Nun, a man in whom is the spirit, and lay your hand upon him.'" (Num 27:18)

Reflection: In the HB (OT) book of Numbers, Moses is instructed by God to lay his hand on the head of Joshua to transfer some of his power and authority to the future leader of the Israelites. In this account, Joshua's spirit already has received the Spirit; Moses transfers some of his authority to him. However, in the CB (NT), the act of laying one's hands on the head of another, as do Peter and John upon those baptized in Samaria who (have not yet received the Spirit) indeed receive the Spirit when the two apostles lay their hands on them (Acts 8:16–19), becomes the sign of giving the Spirit to spirit. Likewise, when Paul reached Ephesus, he discovered that disciples there had not received the Spirit; in fact they had not even heard that there is a Holy Spirit (Acts 19:2). "When Paul had laid his hands on them, the Holy Spirit came upon them ..." (Acts 19:6).

The action of laying hands upon people or things signifies the giving and receiving of the Spirit. This is emphasized in the OC, which explains that after Pentecost filled the apostles with the Spirit, they "transmitted the Spirit to the faithful through the laying on of hands."[15] The bishop or priest imitates Moses in laying his hand upon Joshua; the bishop or priest lays his hand upon the head of each individual person to be confirmed as well as first laying his hands over all those collectively to be confirmed.[16] However, the laying on of hands occurs in all the other six sacraments, too. Before baptizing, the minister lays his hand on each candidate; this occurs multiple times for adults.[17] He lays his hands over bread and wine at every Mass.[18] When celebrating the *Rite of Penance*, the priest or bishop "extends his hands, or at least his right hand, over the head of the penitent,"[19] which he also does when celebrating the anointing

---

15. OC, par. 7.

16. Ibid., pars. 9, 22, 25, 39.

17. *Rite of Baptism for Children*, pars. 51, 88, 115; *Rite of Christian Initiation of Adults*, pars.71, 94, 97, 133, 135, 154, 161, 167, 158, 175, 234, 431, 470, 493, 527, 559, 590.

18. "Order of Mass," pars. 88, 101, 109, 118; "Appendix," Eucharistic Prayers for Reconciliation, I, par. 3; II, par. 3; Eucharistic Prayer for Use in Masses for Various Needs, I, par. 3; II, par. 3; III, par. 3; IV, par 3.

19. *Rite of Penance*, par. 19; cf. pars. 55, 62.

of the sick:[20] "The laying on of hands is . . . an invocation: the Church prays for the coming of the Holy Spirit upon the sick person."[21] In the ordination of a bishop, priest, or deacon, hands are laid on the priest being consecrated a bishop, on the deacon being ordained a priest, or on the man being ordained a deacon.[22] Even when celebrating matrimony, the minister lays hands on the newly-married couple[23] by extending his hands over them to indicate that "the Holy Spirit brings it about that . . . Christian spouses . . . strive to nurture and foster their union in equal dignity, mutual giving, and the undivided love that flows from the divine font of charity."[24] Thus, the giving and receiving of the Spirit is made known when hands are laid upon people or things.

Journal/Meditation: When have you had a bishop, priest, or deacon lay hands upon you to indicate that he was giving you the Spirit and your spirit was receiving the Spirit?

Prayer: Father, through the laying on of hands, the apostles of your Son gave the Spirit to your people. Fill ministers of the gospel with that same Spirit that they, through the laying on of their hands, may fill my spirit. Grant this in the name of Jesus Christ now and forever Amen.

Spirit Fire

Scripture: "Divided tongues, as of fire, appeared among [the apostles], and a tongue rested on each of them. All of them were filled with the Holy Spirit . . . ." (Acts 2:3–4)

Reflection: According to the Acts of the Apostles, on the day of Pentecost, Jesus' apostles experienced the divine presence like fire, just like Abraham did (Gen 15:17), just like Moses did (Exod 3:2; 13:21–22; 24:17), and just like Elijah did (1 Kgs 18:38–39). According to the CCC, "fire symbolizes the transforming energy of the Holy Spirit's actions."[25] Both the author of Matthew's Gospel and the author of Luke's Gospel

---

20. *Pastoral Care of the Sick*, pars. 5, 52, 106, 122, 139, 156.

21. Ibid., par. 106.

22. *Roman Pontifical*, "Ordination of a Bishop," 227, "Ordination of Bishops," 248; "Ordination of Priests," 196, "Ordination of a Priest," 212; "Ordination of Deacons," 164, "Ordination of a Deacon," 182.

23. *Order of Celebrating Matrimony*, pars. 74, 77, 105, 139, 205B, 207, 209.

24. Ibid., par. 9.

25. CCC, par. 696.

portray John the Baptist declaring that Jesus would baptize with the Holy Spirit and fire (Matt 3:11b; Luke 3:16b). In his second volume, the author of Luke's Gospel fulfills John's words with Pentecost. Just like fire transforms whatever it touches, the powerful Spirit connects to spirit and transforms people with his divine self. The ministry of Jesus poured out the fire of the Spirit on the earth.[26] According to the CCC, the metaphor of fire is "one of the most expressive images of the Holy Spirit's actions."[27] This is why the RM refers to the fire Moses experienced on Mount Sinai (Horeb) where the previous covenant was revealed and to the new covenant manifested in the fire of the Spirit on Pentecost.[28] It is also why we pray that the purifying flame that appeared above the apostles will cleanse our hearts of all evil and set us aflame with the Spirit.[29]

Besides transforming whatever it touches, fire also creates light. Thus, the RM often refers to the light of the Holy Spirit—asking God to let the Spirit fill us with the light of faith[30]—and the bright rays of the Holy Spirit.[31] We also often pray to be enlightened by the Holy Spirit,[32] or we acknowledge those who were enlightened by the Spirit.[33] Those who bask in the fire and light of the Spirit are given clarifying information about God, freed from ignorance, and taught a depth of spiritual understanding that transforms them. When Spirit fire touches spirit, transformation is the result.

---

26. OC, pars. 22, 39.

27. CCC, par. 696.

28. "Pentecost Sunday," At the Vigil Mass, Extended Form, par. 6.

29. "Blessings," I. For Celebrations in the Different Liturgical Times, 8. The Holy Spirit, 678; "Pentecost Sunday," At the Vigil Mass, Extended Form, par. 6.

30. "Proper of Time," Easter Time, Friday of the Seventh Week of Easter, Collect, 443; "Proper of Saints," The Conversion of St. Paul the Apostle, January 25, Prayer over the Offerings, 811; St. Ambrose, December 7, Prayer over the Offerings, 1009; "Votive Masses," 9. The Holy Spirit, A, Collect, Prayer over the Offerings, 1338; 10. The Blessed Virgin Mary, C, The Most Holy Name of Mary, Prayer over the Offerings, 1350; 17. St. Paul, Apostle, Prayer over the Offerings, 1364.

31. "Pentecost Sunday," At the Vigil Mass, Simple Form, 451.

32. "Friday of the Passion of the Lord [Good Friday]," par. 13, VII; "Common of the Blessed Virgin Mary," I. In Ordinary Time, 4, Prayer over the Offerings, 1043; "Masses and Prayers," I. For Holy Church, 7. For the Priest Himself, B, Collect, 1253; 17. For the Unity of Christians, C, Collect, 1278; "Votive Masses," 9. The Holy Spirit, B, Collect, 1341.

33. "Proper of Saints," The Presentation of the Lord, February 2, The Blessing of Candles and the Procession, par. 4.

Journal/Meditation: When have you experienced the Spirit like fire? What was the light? How were you enlightened? What transformation occurred?

Prayer: Father, while your Son's apostles were huddled together, you set them on fire with the power of the Spirit. Fill me with that same light and enlighten my mind with the truth that you are one God—Father, Son, and Holy Spirit—forever and ever. Amen.

Spirit Breath

Scripture: "[Jesus] breathed on [his disciples] and said to them, 'Receive the Holy Spirit.'" (John 20:22)

Reflection: While not at first glance as powerful as fire, breath, as a sign of the Spirit, connotes the power of life; without air we die. Because the word *pneuma* in Greek is the same word for breath, air, wind, and spirit, the author of John's Gospel portrays Pentecost taking place on Easter Sunday evening with the appearance of the risen Jesus to his disciples and with his simple action of breathing Spirit on them. Jesus does what the LORD God does to the man he has just formed from the dust of the ground; he "breathed into his nostrils the breath of life; and the man became a living being" (Gen 2:7). Jesus' disciples now become inspired and empowered missionaries.

The action of breathing on another is called insufflation. Today we might better grasp the metaphor with respiration, the process in living organisms involving the production of energy, typically with the intake of oxygen and the release of carbon dioxide—air—from the oxidation of complex organic substances. In other words, the risen Jesus energizes his disciples' spirits with the power of the Spirit's breath, giving them eternal breath. He functions as a modern medical ventilator; he gives them mouth to mouth resuscitation. While breathing on another is considered inappropriate today, there are still at least two occasions where it occurs in the celebration of liturgical rites. First, there is an optional rite—"Exorcism and Renunciation of False Worship"—in the "Rite of Acceptance into the Order of Catechumens" in the *Rite of Christian Initiation of Adults*. The rubrics indicate that "the celebrant breathes lightly toward the face of each candidate" in order to blow away any evil spirit.[34] Second, before consecrating the Chrism Oil, the rubrics state that "the

---

34. *Rite of Christian Initiation of Adults*, par. 71.

bishop may breathe over the opening of the vessel of Chrism" before singing or saying the consecratory prayer, which asks the Father to fill the oil with the power of the Spirit.[35] Thus, all people who are anointed with it are given the power of Spirit breath.

Journal/Meditation: What further insights on the power of Spirit connected to your spirit as breath have you had? How have you breathed Spirit on spirit?

Prayer: Father, on the evening of his resurrection your Son breathed the Spirit on the spirits of his disciples. Blow the life-giving breath of the Spirit upon my spirit that I may proclaim the gospel of Jesus Christ, who with you and the Holy Spirit lives and reigns forever and ever. Amen.

Spirit and Power

Scripture: The angel said to Zechariah: "With the spirit and power of Elijah [John the Baptist] will go before [the Lord], to turn the hearts of parents to their children, and the disobedient to the wisdom of the righteous, to make ready a people prepared for the Lord." (Luke 1:17)

Reflection: The angel Gabriel, who visits Zechariah in the Jerusalem Temple, tells him that the child to be born to him and his wife, Elizabeth, in their old age will be filled with the Holy Spirit (Luke 1:15), just like Elijah was full of the Lord's Spirit. In the HB (OT) First Book of Kings this is voiced by Obadiah, who tells the prophet, "As soon as I have gone from you, the spirit of the LORD will carry you I know not where" (1 Kgs 18:12). This is also attested by Elisha, Elijah's successor, who asks Elijah to let him "inherit a double share of [his] spirit" (2 Kgs 2:9). And after Elijah ascends in a whirlwind into heaven, this is attested by the company of prophets, who tell Elisha that "it may be that the spirit of the Lord has caught [Elijah] up and thrown him down on some mountain or into some valley" (2 Kgs 2:16). The author of Luke's Gospel presents John the Baptist as Elijah returned (cf. Mal 4:5–6 [3:19–24]); his spirit is animated by the same powerful Spirit as the ancient prophet.

In both Elijah's world and John the Baptist's world, everyone presumed a three-storied universe. The earth, where people lived, was considered to be in the middle. Above the dome of the sky was heaven, where God lived. And under the earth, Sheol, was where the dead lived. This is why Elijah goes from the earth to heaven in a whirlwind that is like

---

35. *Order of Blessing the Oil of Catechumens*, par. 25.

a tornado connecting the two levels of earth and heaven. Since heaven, where God lives, is up, he must send down the Spirit to earth. Thus, in the RM, God is asked to send down the Spirit on the gifts of bread and wine,[36] or to send forth the Spirit to sanctify the gifts of bread and wine,[37] just like Jesus sent the Holy Spirit from the Father as the first fruits for believers.[38] The spirit of Elijah lives on those who have welcomed the Spirit to connect to their spirits.

Journal/Meditation: In what specific way have you experienced the Spirit and power of Elijah? How has the Spirit and spirit of Elijah touched your spirit?

Prayer: With the spirit and power of Elijah, Father, you sent John the Baptist to prepare the way for the coming of your Son. Send down your Spirit on my spirit that I may recognize the wisdom of the righteous and one day ascend to your divine presence. You are one God—Father, Son, and Holy Spirit—forever and ever. Amen.

Anointing Spirit

Scripture: "[Andrew] first found his brother Simon and said to him, 'We have found the Messiah' (which is translated Anointed)." (John 1:41)

Reflection: In order to understand the various levels of meaning in the above verse from John's Gospel, the reader must know that the Hebrew word for anointed is *messiah*, and the Greek word for anointed is *christ*. While both words are used as descriptions of Jesus, they mean that he is one chosen by God for a specific purpose: to reveal who God is. Jesus is the anointed because the Spirit descended upon him and remained in him; he baptizes with the Holy Spirit, according to John's Gospel (1:33). His last name is not Messiah (as in Jesus Messiah) or Christ (as in Jesus Christ). He has no last name. The words *messiah* and *christ* designate his mission to reveal the God who offers people eternal life. He comes into the world from God and is anointed with the fullness of life by the Spirit.

The CCC states that Jesus is God's anointed in a unique way; his entire humanity was anointed with the Spirit. In other words, the Spirit

---

36. "Order of Mass," par. 101.

37. "Appendix," Eucharistic Prayer for Use in Masses for Various Needs, I, par. 3; II, par. 3; III, par. 3; IV, par. 3.

38. "Order of Mass," par. 117.

established him as the Christ, the Anointed.[39] Thus, the RM proclaims that God anointed his only-begotten Son with the Holy Spirit[40] and made him high priest of the new covenant.[41] Those who are confirmed are declared to be anointed with the Holy Spirit[42] or to have received a spiritual anointing.[43] According to the CCC, "The symbolism of anointing with oil . . . signifies the Holy Spirit, to the point of becoming a synonym for the Holy Spirit."[44] The power of the Spirit is given to the spirit through the action of anointing with Chrism, which gets its name from Christ, the Anointed.

Journal/Meditation: How many times have you been anointed? Make a list and identify what power the Spirit gave to your spirit.

Prayer: Almighty God, you anointed your only-begotten Son with the Spirit. Anoint my spirit with that same Spirit that I may be conformed more and more to Jesus Christ, who lives and reigns with you forever and ever. Amen.

Spiritual Seal

Scripture: ". . . [I]t is God who establishes us with you in Christ and has anointed us, by putting his seal on us and giving us his Spirit in our hearts as a first installment." (2 Cor 1:22)

Reflection: A seal is a closure that prevents the entrance or escape of something. It can also be an authenticating stamp with a raised emblem that is pressed into wax or touched to an ink pad and then stamped onto paper. Both of these meanings of the word *seal* are found in the above verse from Paul's Second Letter to the Corinthians. According to

---

39. CCC, par. 695.

40. "Thursday of Holy Week [Holy Thursday], The Chrism Mass," par. 7; "Easter Sunday," pars. 44, 46.

41. "Thursday of Holy Week [Holy Thursday], The Chrism Mass," par. 12; "Ritual Masses," IV. For the Conferral of Holy Orders, 1. For the Ordination of a Bishop, A, Preface, 1140; 2. For the Ordination of Priests, A, Preface, 1153; B, 1158; 3. For the Ordination of Deacons, A, Preface, 1162–1164; B, 1169.

42. "Ritual Masses," I. For the Conferral of the Sacraments of Christian Initiation, 4. For the Conferral of Confirmation, A, Prayer after Communion, 1131; OC, A, Prayer after Communion, par. 58.

43. "Ritual Masses," I. For the Conferral of the Sacraments of Christian Initiation, 4. For the Conferral of Confirmation, B, Prayer over the Offerings, 1133; OC, B, Prayer over the Offerings, par. 59.

44. CCC, par. 695.

the apostle, God has set a closure on those who believe that Jesus is his Son, and he has authenticated them with the stamp of the Spirit. The author of the Letter to the Ephesians puts it this way: "In [Christ] you also, when you had heard the word of truth, the gospel of your salvation, and had believed in him, were marked with the seal of the promised Holy Spirit" (Eph 1:13). The same author later in the letter refers to the Holy Spirit of God with which the Ephesians were marked with a seal for the day of redemption (Eph 4:30). The Johannine Jesus refers to himself as the one on whom God has set his seal (John 6:27).

The CCC states, "... [S]eal indicates the indelible effect of the anointing with the Holy Spirit in the sacraments of baptism, confirmation, and holy orders ...."[45] This means that these sacraments are unrepeatable. The RM refers to this unrepeatability as being signed with the seal of the Spirit.[46] While being anointed with Chrism—which is perfumed olive oil insufflated with the Spirit—to each person being confirmed the minister says, "Be sealed with the gift of the Holy Spirit."[47] It is a spiritual seal by which those who are anointed are conformed to Christ.[48] This is clearly stated in the introduction to the OC: "Signed with the perfumed oil ..., the baptized receive the indelible character, the seal of the Lord, together with the gift of the Spirit that conforms them more fully to Christ ...."[49] The powerful Spirit is given to spirit as both a closure and an indelible stamp that identifies one as Christ.

Journal/Meditation: If you have been baptized, confirmed, or ordained, how do you manifest the seal of the Spirit that conforms you to Christ? If you have not been baptized, confirmed, or ordained, how do you see those who have received the seal of the Spirit manifesting Christ?

Prayer: O God, you establish your people in Christ and anoint them by putting your seal on them and giving them your Spirit. Renew your gift of the Spirit in my heart and conform me even more to the image of Christ, your Son, who lives and reigns with you and the Holy Spirit, one God, forever and ever. Amen.

---

45. Ibid., par. 698.
46. "Appendix," Eucharistic Prayer for Use in Masses for Various Needs, III, par. 1.
47. OC, pars. 27, 44, 55, 56.
48. Ibid., pars. 22, 39.
49. Ibid., par. 9.

Adoptive Spirit

Scripture: ". . . [Y]ou did not receive a spirit of slavery to fall back into fear, but you have received a spirit of adoption. When we cry, 'Abba! Father!' it is that very Spirit bearing witness with our spirit that we are children of God." (Rom 8:15–16)

Reflection: Adoption is the act of raising a child of other biological parents as if he or she were one's own. When Paul uses the phrase *spirit of adoption*, he means that God has chosen people for himself through Christ. Just like God adopted the Israelites at one moment in history (Rom 9:4), now, through Christ, God has adopted all people as children. Indeed, "all who are led by the Spirit of God are children of God" (Rom 8:14). We have the first fruits of the Spirit (Rom 8:23) through Christ. And because we are children, "God has sent the Spirit of his Son into our hearts, crying, 'Abba! Father!'" (Gal 4:5–6) The author of the Letter to the Ephesians, states, "[God] destined us for adoption as his children through Jesus Christ, according to the good pleasure of his will" (Eph 1:5). It is the Spirit who adopts our spirits and enables us to call upon God as Abba or Father.

The Collect of the Easter Vigil asks God to stir up a spirit of adoption in the church.[50] At the conclusion of the Litany of Saints, the ever-living God is asked to send forth the spirit of adoption to create new people in the baptismal font,[51] and that we, strengthened by the spirit of adoption, may walk in newness of life.[52] He is also requested to sanctify by the spirit of adoption his children, whom he feeds with the eucharistic body of his Son.[53] When Spirit connects to spirit, we call out like children to their male parent: Abba, Father, or Daddy. If Paul were writing today, he'd add the female parent, too: Emm (or Immah), Mother, or Mommy. The powerful Spirit adopts spirit, and we cannot help but be children, saying, Father or Mother.

Journal/Meditation: What are the immediate implications for you of calling God Father and Mother? How have you experienced the spirit of adoption by the Spirit?

---

50. "Easter Sunday, par. 32."

51. Ibid., par. 43.

52. "Ritual Masses," I. For the Conferral of the Sacraments of Christian Initiation, 3. For the Conferral of Baptism, A, Collect, 1126.

53. "Proper of Saints," Sts. Joachim and Anne, July 26, Prayer after Communion, 909.

Prayer: Father, stir up a spirit of adoption among all your people so that strengthened by the Spirit they may always walk in newness life. Abba, hear my prayer in the name of your Son, Jesus Christ, who named you Father now and forever. Amen.

Temple of Spirit

Scripture: "... [D]o you not know that your body is a temple of the Holy Spirit within you, which you have from God, and that you are not your own?" (1 Cor 6:19)

Reflection: In the ancient world, a temple of any kind was the place where a god dwelled. In the HB (OT), the LORD was thought to dwell in the Temple in Jerusalem; however, other religions had temples and shrines in which worshipers thought their god(s) lived. In his First Letter to the Corinthians, Paul, employing the temple metaphor, asks his readers if they are unaware that they are like a temple in which dwells the Spirit. Earlier in the same letter, he asked: "Do you not know that you are God's temple and that God's Spirit dwells in you?" (1 Cor 3:16) In other words, each person is a temple-spirit in which lives the Spirit. Of course, this is not a new metaphor. In the HB (OT) book of Job, Elihu states that the spirit within him constrains him (Job 32:18). Joseph, son of Jacob, is described by Pharaoh as one in whom is the spirit of God (Gen 41:38), and the prophet Daniel is described by King Belshazzar as possessing a spirit of the gods (Dan 5:14). The prophet Isaiah recounts one of the LORD's mighty deeds as putting his holy spirit within his people (Isa 63:11), while the prophet Ezekiel presents God declaring that he will put a new spirit within his people (Ezek 36:26–27). In the CB (NT), the author of the Second Letter to Timothy exhorts his readers to guard the treasure entrusted to them, that is, the Spirit living in them (2 Tim 1:14), while the author of the First Letter of Peter refers to the Spirit of Christ within (1 Pet 1;11).

There are multiple references to the individual being the temple or dwelling place of the Spirit in the RM. God is asked to make his children a temple and a dwelling place of the Spirit,[54] and a perfect temple of his

---

54. "Blessings," III. Other Blessings, 19. For the Dedication of a Church, 684; "Common of the Dedication of a Church," On the Anniversary of the Dedication, I. In the Church that was Dedicated, Blessing, 1035; "Ritual Masses," X. For the Dedication of a Church and an Altar, 1. For the Dedication of a Church, Blessing, 1227.

glory with the gracious dwelling of the Holy Spirit.[55] God is attributed with preparing a fit dwelling place for the Spirit in the heart of Mary, and he is asked to make us a worthy temple of his glory.[56] We declare that God perfects us as temples of the Spirit,[57] and we ask that we may in spirit dwell already in the heavenly temple.[58] God's Spirit is so close to our spirit that they are one and the same. The Spirit dwells in us like gods live in temples. Spirit indwelling spirit makes us temples of Spirit and spirit. We can answer the question about knowing that our bodies are temples of the Holy Spirit posed by Paul to the Corinthians by answering that we do know this. Because powerful Spirit dwells in spirit, we also know that we are not our own; we belong to God.

Journal/Meditation: In what specific ways have you experienced yourself as a temple in which the Spirit dwells? What response do you make?

Prayer: Heavenly Father, graciously continue to perfect the union of your Spirit and my spirit. By making me a dwelling place for your Spirit you enable my spirit to praise your glory from my temple now and forever. Amen.

Work of the Spirit

Scripture: "The only thing I want to learn from you is this: Did you receive the Spirit by doing the works of the law or by believing what you heard? Are you so foolish? Having started with the Spirit, are you now ending with the flesh? Did you experience so much for nothing?—if it really was for nothing. Well then, does God supply you with the Spirit and work miracles among you by your doing the works of the law, or by your believing what you heard?" (Gal 3:2–5)

---

55. "Proper of Time," Easter Time, Tuesday of the Seventh Week of Easter, Collect, 440; "Ritual Masses," I. For the Conferral of the Sacraments of Christian Initiation, 4. For the Conferral of Confirmation, Collect, 1130; OC, pars. 35, 58.

56. "Proper of Saints," Immaculate Heart of the Blessed Virgin Mary, Saturday after the Second Sunday after Pentecost, Collect, 869.

57. "Proper of Saints," Dedication of the Lateran Basilica, November 9, Preface, 988–990; "Common of the Dedication of a Church," On the Anniversary of the Dedication, II. Outside the Church that was Dedicated, Preface, 1037.

58. "Proper of Time," Easter Time, Ascension of the Lord, At the Mass during the Day, Collect, 432.

Reflection: According to Paul in his Second Letter to the Corinthians, "The signs of a true apostle were performed among [them] with utmost patience, signs and wonders and mighty works" (2 Cor 12:12). In his Letter to the Romans, he writes, ". . . I will not venture to speak of anything except what Christ has accomplished through me to win obedience from the Gentiles, by word and deed, by the power of signs and wonders, by the power of the Spirit of God, so that from Jerusalem and as far around as Illyricum I have fully proclaimed the good news of Christ" (Rom 15:18–19). In other words, "the beginnings [of the Most High] are manifest in wonders and mighty works" (2 Esd 9:6). For Paul the mark of the beginning of genuine conversion to Christ is the experience of God's life-giving Spirit dwelling within (Rom 8:9). The working of miracles signifies the presence of the Spirit (1 Cor 12:10).

With such background, we are now able to answer the questions Paul asks in the four verses above from his Letter to the Galatians. First, Paul asks the Galatians if they received the Spirit by doing the works of the law or by believing what they heard. The answer is by believing the good news of Christ that he preached. Second, he asks the Galatians if God supplies them with the Spirit to work miracles by doing the works of the law or by believing what they heard. The answer is by believing what they heard and remembering the signs, wonders, and mighty works that the Spirit accomplished through Paul and through them. Paul does not want the Galatians to return to works of the law in an attempt to earn salvation; he wants their spirits to continue to be the means for the Spirit to do mighty works in the salvation offered freely to them through Christ Jesus. Otherwise, they demonstrate their foolishness! (Gal 3:1, 3a) They experienced the mighty works of the powerful Spirit for nothing.

Journal/Meditation: What mighty work has the Spirit done through your spirit?

Prayer: By the will of your Father and the work of the Holy Spirit, Lord Jesus Christ, you gave life to the world through your death and resurrection. Supply my spirit with the Spirit to do the mighty work of announcing your gospel. You are Lord forever and ever. Amen.

Drink the Spirit

Scripture: ". . . [I]n the one Spirit we were all baptized into one body—Jews or Greeks, slaves or free—and we were all made to drink of one Spirit." (1 Cor 12:13)

Reflection: After listing the Spirit's many activities manifested as spiritual gifts in his First Letter to the Corinthians (12:1–11), Paul declares that through common baptism, all—Jews and Gentiles—drink of the one Spirit. The powerful Spirit is at work in the spirits of the baptized. Through baptism a person experiences spirit being imbued with Spirit; it is like drinking the finest French Merlot or Argentinean Malbec from the same cup. The one Spirit of God connects to all human spirits who have been buried with Christ by baptism into death and raised from the dead to newness of life (Rom 6:3–4). Earlier in the First Letter to the Corinthians, Paul reminds his readers that their ancestors "all drank the same spiritual drink" (1 Cor 10:4). In Pauline understanding, the water they drank from the rock after the exodus (Exod 17:1–7; Num 20:2–13) flowed from the spiritual rock of Christ (1 Cor 10:4). Paul presumes that Christ was preexistent, but now he has been revealed through his death and resurrection. By naming the water-gushing rock spiritual, Paul describes a reality that is thoroughly influenced by the Spirit, who is both the creative and salvific power of God. The metaphor of drinking of the Spirit is used in Job for his spirit. He says, ". . . [T]he arrows of the Almighty are in me; my spirit drinks their poison" (Job 6:4).

In the RM, this metaphor of drinking the Spirit is found in only one Preface. After dedicating a new altar the minister declares that from it believers drink of God's Spirit; the streams flow from Christ, the spiritual rock.[59] Because there is to be only one altar in a church, all drink of one Spirit, who consecrates the elements of bread and wine placed on the altar. All share the one cup of wine, which the Spirit has changed into the blood of Christ. Thus, drinking the one cup is drinking the one Spirit. The altar is Christ, the spiritual rock, who calls upon the Spirit to change the bread and wine on the altar into his body and blood and gives himself, the Father, and the Spirit—Trinity—as powerful spiritual drink. All who enjoy this spiritual drink becoming living altars.

Journal/Meditation: In what specific experiences have you drank of the one Spirit? What was the result of each?

---

59. "Ritual Masses," X. For the Dedication of a Church and an Altar, 2. For the Dedication of an Altar, Preface, 1230–1232.

Prayer: In your one Spirit, Father, all are baptized into one body and all are made to drink of one Spirit. Continue to make my spirit rich with your Spirit. I ask this through my Lord Jesus Christ, who lives and reigns with you and the Holy Spirit, one God, forever and ever. Amen.

Without Spirit

Scripture: "So now deal with me as you will [, O Lord]; command my spirit to be taken from me, so that I may be released from the face of the earth and become dust. For it is better for me to die than to live . . . . Command, O Lord, that I be released from this distress; release me to go to the eternal home . . . . For it is better for me to die than to see so much distress in my life . . . ." (Tob 3:6)

Reflection: When the verse of the above prayer is voiced, Tobit is blind. The OT (A) book of Tobit is a novella spanning fourteen chapters and featuring Tobit, a righteous man who is a captive of Assyria in Nineveh; his wife, Anna; his son, Tobias; the angel, Raphael disguised as Azariah; Sarah, Tobias's future wife; and Sarah's parents, Raguel and Edna. After becoming blind, Tobit prays that God will take away his spirit so that he can return to the ground as dust from which he was made (Gen 3:19). However, he does not think that death is the end; he desires to go to an eternal home even though Raphael promises that God will heal him (Tob 5:10). The point to be focused on here is how the powerful Spirit gives life to spirit, and ancient people described Spirit leaving spirit as death. This is reflected in the HB (OT) book of Joshua. The narrator states that when certain kings "heard that the LORD had dried up the waters of the Jordan for the Israelites until they had crossed over, their hearts melted, and there was no longer any spirit in them, because of the Israelites" (Josh 5:1).

Similarly, "When the queen of Sheba had observed all the wisdom of Solomon, the house that he had built, the food of his table, the seating of his officials, and the attendance of his servants, their clothing, his valets, and his burnt offerings that he offered at the house of the LORD, there was no more spirit in her" (1Kgs 10:4–5; 2 Chr 9:3–4). Even Psalm 76 declares that the LORD "cuts off the spirit of princes" (Ps 76:12), but Psalm 104 states that when the LORD takes away the breath, the spirit, of all he has created, they die and return to their dust (Ps 104:29). It is not until the CB (NT) that the understanding emerges that Spirit connected to spirit preserves spirit from death. In the HB (OT), this is hinted in such texts as Job 19:25–27; Isaiah 25:8a; and Daniel 12:2. In the OT (A), this is hinted in such texts as Wisdom 3:1–4; 4:14; and 2 Maccabees 12:43–44. However, in the CB (NT), it is primarily Paul who writes about spirit being animated by Spirit in this life into eternal life (Rom 6:3–11; 8:12–17) and the book of Revelation (14:13). One way to think about the Spirit connected to and giving life to spirit is the metaphor of a ventilator. This machine moves breathable air into and out of the lungs of a patient who is unable to breathe in order to preserve life. The ventilator is like the Spirit connected to the spirit of the patient keeping him or her alive. The powerful Spirit is like a lifeline, a safety cable, a vital link, connecting God (Spirit) to people (spirit).

Journal/Meditation: What is your first response to Tobit's prayer that God command his spirit to be taken from him? Which metaphor for Spirit connected to spirit—ventilator, lifeline, safety cable, vital link—best describes the life-giving and life-preserving role of the Holy Spirit for you? Explain.

Prayer: Deal with me as you will, O Lord, but do not take your Spirit from me. When I am released from the face of the earth and become dust, command my spirit to be fully united to the Holy Spirit, who with you, Father, and your Son, Jesus Christ, are one God forever and ever. Amen.

5

Spiritual Results

Promised Spirit

Scripture: ". . . [I]n Christ Jesus the blessing of Abraham [has] come to the Gentiles, so that we might receive the promise of the Spirit through faith." (Gal 3:14)

Reflection: There is no doubt in Paul's Letter to the Galatians that his Gentile readers have received the Spirit through their faith that God raised Jesus from the dead (Gal 3:2, 5). Through their faith, Gentiles are descendants of Abraham, who received the gospel beforehand when God said, "All the Gentiles shall be blessed in you" (Gal 3:8). Thus, all believers—Jews or Gentiles—are blessed, and that blessing is the reception of the promised Spirit, mediated through faith. The author of the Letter to the Ephesians summarizes this Pauline point, writing: "In [Christ] you also, when you had heard the word of truth, the gospel of your salvation, and had believed in him, were marked with the seal of the promised Holy Spirit" (Eph 1:13).

In the Acts, the not-yet-ascended Jesus tells his apostles "to wait . . . for the promise of the Father" (Acts 1:4) which is identified as baptism by the Holy Spirit (Acts 1:5). The promise is fulfilled with Pentecost (Acts 2:1–4). The minister's address during the Pentecost Vigil Mass mentions awaiting the Spirit promised by God.[1] The Solemn Blessing at the end

---

1. "Pentecost Sunday," At the Vigil Mass, Extended Form, par. 3.

of Confirmation wishes true faith to the newly confirmed from the Son, who promised that the Spirit of truth would abide in the church,[2] while Preface I of the Holy Spirit declares that the Son poured out the promised Spirit on God's adopted children.[3] And another Preface mentions that the mother of Jesus, Mary, joined the apostles awaiting the promised Spirit.[4] A promise is assurance that something will certainly happen. A divine promise is a pledge made to Abraham, according to Paul, and fulfilled in all who believe with the Spirit given to all people. This results in Spirit connected to spirit.

Journal/Meditation: How has the promised Spirit been received by you? What experience(s) of your life lead(s) you to think this?

Prayer: Life-giving God, you draw ever closer to yourself those who persevere in prayer and await the Spirit promised by your Son. Give me a quiet heart to hear your word and to reflect on your great deeds that your Spirit may bring to perfection your will in me. I ask this in the name of Jesus Christ my Lord. Amen.

Spiritual Perception

Scripture: "At once Jesus perceived in his spirit that [the scribes] were discussing these questions ["Why does this fellow speak in this way? Who can forgive sins but God alone?" (Mark 2:7)] among themselves; and he said to them, 'Why do you raise such questions in your hearts?'" (Mark 2:8)

Reflection: According to the author of Mark's Gospel, Jesus noticed something that escaped the awareness of others; in his spirit he perceived the questions the scribes were thinking after he had healed a paralyzed man by forgiving him his sins (Mark 2:1–5). The Markan Jesus does not possess extrasensory perception. His spirit is connected intimately to the universal Spirit, who communicates important information to him. This same idea is also found in Paul's First Letter to the Corinthians. The apostle tells his readers that though he is absent in body he is present in spirit (1 Cor 5:3). He can write this because his spirit is connected to

---

2. "Ritual Masses," I. For the Conferral of the Sacraments of Christian Initiation, 4. For the Conferral of Confirmation, A, Solemn Blessing, 1132; OC, pars. 33, 49.

3. "Votive Masses," 9. The Holy Spirit, A, Preface, 1339–1340.

4. Ibid., 10. The Blessed Virgin Mary, B. Our Lady, Mother of the Church, Preface, 1346–1348.

Spirit, which is connected to the spirits of the Corinthians. "When you are assembled, . . . my spirit is present with the power of our Lord Jesus," Paul writes (1 Cor 5:4b). Then, addressing the issue of a man in the community living with his father's wife (1 Cor 5:1), Paul tells the Corinthians that their task is to save his spirit for the day of the Lord (1 Cor 5:5). That can only be done, of course, if spirit remains connected to Spirit.

In the HB (OT), Job loathes his life and speaks the bitterness of his suffering, but he also acknowledge that God's care has preserved his spirit (Job 10:12). This has occurred because it is God who fashioned Job like clay, and it is God who will turn him to dust again (Job 10:9). But it is also true that it is God's Spirit that animates Job's spirit, and God's Spirit preserves all spirit to which it is connected. The author of Mark's Gospel presents Jesus' spirit being so connected that he knows the questions the scribes are thinking. Paul can write to the Corinthians that he is present in spirit—even though bodily absent—because his spirit is connected to Spirit, which is connected to the spirits of the Corinthians. And in his misery, Job knows that God has preserved his spirit with Spirit; he just doesn't know what purpose his extreme suffering serves. We, however, know that the Spirit is present to keep us safe all the time.[5]

Journal/Meditation: When have you perceived in your spirit the Spirit connecting you in some way to another? When have you perceived in your spirit the Spirit connecting you in some way to a community?

Prayer: Almighty God, your Spirit is present to your people, keeping them safe, all the time. Give me a greater awareness of your care that preserves my spirit until the day of Christ Jesus, who lives with you in perfect Trinity—Father, Son, and Holy Spirit—forever and ever. Amen.

Spiritual Endowment

Scripture: "At last Daniel came in before me [, Nebuchadnezzar,]—he who was named Belteshazzar after the name of my god, and who is endowed with a spirit of the holy gods—and I told him the dream." (Dan 4:8)

Reflection: The verse above from the HB (OT) book of Daniel is only one of several that present the Jewish exile as endowed with the spirit of the holy gods or a holy, divine spirit. While already touched upon

---

5. "Appendices," Appendix II: Rite for the Blessing and Sprinkling of Water, par. 3.

above, we want to explore deeply the spiritual endowment theme here. In the prologue to Nebuchadnezzar's narration of his dream to Daniel, he again states that the prophet is "endowed with a spirit of the holy gods" (Dan 4:9), and after narrating the dream he states that Daniel is "endowed with a spirit of the holy gods" (Dan 4:18). In the next narration of another dream by regent Belshazzar, his wife tells him, "There is a man in your kingdom who is endowed with a spirit of the holy gods" (Dan 5:11a). The Spirit with which Daniel is endowed enables him to interpret the dreams of his royal captors, but it also gives him the reputation of being a wise man faithful to his God in Babylonian exile. Through the dreams he interprets, he reveals God's will.

Once a person is endowed with the Spirit, he or she can also be said to be trustworthy in spirit and can keep a confidence (Prov 11:13), unlike the stubborn whose spirit is not faithful to God (Ps 78:8). The psalmist sings, "Into your hand I commit my spirit; you have redeemed me, O LORD, faithful God" (Ps 31:5). In the RM, we petition God to renew us so we can remain faithful to the Spirit with whom we are endowed.[6] Echoing Psalm 31:5, we also pray that we can entrust ourselves more fully to the Spirit which will enable our spirits to turn back to God.[7] We have been provided the Spirit, who connects to our spirits, like the Spirit connected to Daniel's spirit. While we may not be responsible for interpreting dreams, our spiritual endowment gives us the ability to discern God's will for ourselves and for others.

Journal/Meditation: What is your spiritual endowment? What will of God has it enabled you to discern for yourself? for others?

Prayer: Into your hand I commit my spirit, O LORD; you have redeemed me, faithful God. Keep my spirit faithful to the Spirit and enable me to entrust myself more fully to you, who are one God—Father, Son, and Holy Spirit—forever and ever. Amen.

Spiritual Sharing

Scripture: ". . . [T]he LORD came down in the cloud and spoke to [Moses], and took some of the spirit that was on him and put it on the seventy elders . . . ." (Num 11:25a)

---

6. "Easter Sunday," par. 54.
7. "Appendix," Eucharistic Prayers for Reconciliation, I, par. 1.

Reflection: Another spiritual result of Spirit connected to spirit is sharing Spirit and spirit. This is demonstrated in the HB (OT) book of Numbers in the narrative about Moses appointing seventy (-two) elders to help him govern the Israelites. The LORD had told Moses, "I will come down and talk with you . . . ; and I will take some of the spirit that is on you and put it on [the elders] . . ." (Num 11:17). A similar scene is narrated in the Second Book of Kings. The prophet Elisha says to Elijah, who is about to be taken into heaven in a whirlwind, "Please let me inherit a double share of your spirit" (2 Kgs 2:9). The fact that Elisha shares Elijah's spirit is confirmed by the company of prophets, who declare, "The spirit of Elijah rests on Elisha" (2 Kgs 2:15). Even though we may be animated, like Elisha, with a borrowed spirit (Wis 15:16), we can, according to Paul, "stand firm in the one spirit, striving side by side with one mind for the faith of the gospel" (Phil 1:27). Later, Paul will specifically refer to "sharing in the Spirit" (Phil 2:1). Because of the strong ties between Spirit and spirits, the author of the Letter to the Hebrews does not think that it is possible "to restore again to repentance those who have once been enlightened, and have tasted the heavenly gift, and have shared in the Holy Spirit, and have tasted the goodness of the word of God and the powers of the age to come, and then have fallen away . . ." (Heb 6:4–6). Later generations will disagree with the Hebrews' author and decree that what we have or use in common with others can be restored.

While Spirit is divided and shared with spirit, it is not diminished. While Spirit is divided and shared with spirit, it is not disconnected. To say that we can disconnect our spirit from Spirit is to give us more power than God. We experience divided and shared Spirit and spirit when engaged in worship that lifts us into the realm of the sacred through song, gestures, and words. We also experience the divided and shared Spirit and spirit when attending sports events like football, baseball, and basketball; people share Spirit and spirit through their chants, their standing up and sitting down, and their shouts of encouragement to the players of the sport. Family meals are occasions for spirit and Spirit to be shared through food, a common table, and conversation. Spiritual sharing of spirit with spirit mirrors God's sharing of Spirit with our spirits.

Journal/Meditation: When did you last engage in spiritual sharing? With whose spirit did you share spirit? How was Spirit shared through sharing spirit?

Prayer: Taking some of the Spirit you bestowed upon your servant Moses, O LORD, you shared it with the elders chosen to help lead the

Israelites. Grant me a generous sharing of your Spirit that I may, in turn, share spirit with others. I ask this in the name of Jesus Christ, your Son, who is Lord with you and the Holy Spirit now and forever. Amen.

Spiritual Accompaniment

Scripture: Elisha said to Gehazi, "Did I not go with you in spirit when someone left his chariot to meet you?" (2 Kgs 5:26a)

Reflection: Following the long narrative about Naaman and Elisha in the HB (OT) Second Book of Kings, Elisha confronts his servant, Gehazi, about soliciting gifts from Naaman after Elisha refused to accept anything. Gehazi is unaware that Elisha has accompanied him in spirit; Elisha has traveled with Gehazi, knows what he did, and has now trapped him in a lie. Elisha illustrates what Paul will write about in his First Letter to the Corinthians. Spiritual accompaniment, like all other spiritual gifts, is "activated by one and the same Spirit, who allots to each one individually just as the Spirit chooses" (1 Cor 12:11). Because Spirit connects to spirit, Elisha can accompany Gehazi in spirit.

In Luke's Gospel, John the Baptist is declared to be "strong in spirit" (Luke 1:80), but in his preaching he declares that there is coming one more powerful than he who will baptize with the Holy Spirit and fire (Luke 3:16). In other words, John the Baptist's strength in Spirit accompanies him in announcing the one who will be so strong in Spirit that he will baptize with it. The baptism in Spirit occurs in Luke's second volume, the Acts of the Apostles, with his unique narration of Pentecost and the divided tongues of fire that appear and rest on all gathered in an upstairs room (Acts 2:1–4). Those who are accompanied by the Spirit need "not to be quickly shaken in mind or alarmed, either by spirit or by word or by letter ... to the effect that the day of the Lord is already here" (2 Thess 2:2). God, who shows both a father's and mother's care for all, accompanies people with his Spirit, uniting them by a fraternal and maternal spirit into a single family of humankind.[8] Spirit accompanies spirit, and spirit accompanies spirit, too.

Journal/Meditation: When have you been accompanied by Spirit? When you have been accompanied by spirit? When have you accompanied a spirit with your spirit?

---

8. "Masses and Prayers," II. For Civil Needs, 30. For the Preservation of Peace and Justice, Collect, 1297.

Prayer: Almighty God, you have given the members of the human race a single origin through the Holy Spirit. Keep all of us united in spirit until the day of the Lord Jesus Christ occurs. He lives and reigns with you, Father, and the Holy Spirit, one God, forever and ever. Amen.

Spiritual Sanctification

Scripture: ". . . [W]e must always give thanks to God for you, brothers and sisters beloved by the Lord, because God chose you as the first fruits for salvation through sanctification by the Spirit and through belief in the truth." (2 Thess 2:13)

Reflection: In the verse above, the author of the Second Letter to the Thessalonians echoes his hero, Paul, who writes about the faith of the Gentiles being acceptable to God and sanctified by the Holy Spirit (Rom 15:16). Another echo of the same idea is found in the First Letter of Peter which is addressed to those "who have been chosen and destined by God the Father and sanctified by the Spirit to be obedient to Jesus Christ . . ." (1 Pet 1:2). Those who are sanctified by the Spirit in Second Thessalonians, Romans, and First Peter are made holy, that is, they share in the very being of God. Spirit connects to spirit and makes it holy, sacred to the Divine. That is why the word *Holy* is placed before the word *Spirit*. The Holy Spirit makes holy every spirit it touches. Paul notes his "holiness of spirit" (2 Cor 6:6) and the holiness in body and spirit of unmarried women and virgins (1 Cor 7:34). Even the author of the First Letter of Peter tells his readers that those who brought the gospel to them did so by the Holy Spirit (1: Pet 1:12).

Before the CB (NT), the author of the OT (A) book of Wisdom stated, ". . . [A] holy and disciplined spirit will flee from deceit, and will leave foolish thoughts behind, and will be ashamed at the approach of unrighteousness" (Wis 1:5). In other words, deceit, foolish thoughts, and unrighteousness are incompatible with the holiness of the spirit touched by Spirit. Before baptisms are done, in the RM God is asked to let the water in the font receive the Holy Spirit,[9] who will make the water holy and make holy (remove deceit, foolish thoughts, and unrighteousness) the spirits of all who are baptized in it. The Lord is asked to sanctify the bread and wine of Eucharist with the Holy Spirit[10] because this is the

---

9. "Easter Sunday," pars. 44, 46.

10. "Order of Mass," par. 118; "Proper of Time," Advent, Fourth Sunday of Advent,

work of the Spirit of sanctification[11] gained for us by God's Son.[12] When dedicating a new altar, we pray that the Holy Spirit will come down upon the new altar to sanctify the gifts of bread and wine.[13] It is the Holy Spirit who enables us to carry out with one accord the works of holiness and life.[14] Spiritual sanctification, the melding of Spirit and spirit, brings us face to face with the invisible Holy One. After this encounter, we are left holy, sacred, and sanctified.

Journal/Meditation: How would you describe the sanctification you have received from the Spirit? What encounter with holiness have you had? What were the results?

Prayer: I must always give thanks to you, O God, for choosing me to be among the first fruits for salvation through sanctification by the Spirit. Keep me sanctified by the Spirit and obedient to your Son, Jesus Christ, that I may share in your divine being now and into eternity. Amen.

Spiritual Unity

Scripture: "... [A]ll of you, have unity of spirit...." (1 Pet 3:8)

Reflection: The result of the unity of spirits and the unity of spirits and Spirit is a greater binding together of the members of the community. Isaiah declares that it is the LORD's spirit who gathers all into unity (Isa 34:16b). The author of the Letter to the Ephesians tells his readers to make "every effort to maintain the unity of the Spirit in the bond of peace" because "[t]here is one body and one Spirit" (Eph 4:3–4), and readers have access in one Spirit to the Father through Christ Jesus (Eph 2:18). At the end of his Second Letter to the Corinthians Paul wishes his readers "the communion of the Holy Spirit" (2 Cor 13:13), while at the end of his Letter to the Galatians, he wishes his readers' spirits the grace of the Lord Jesus Christ (Gal 6:18). The Spirit engenders a spiritual closeness with God and with all other spirits. The result of combining all into

---

Prayer over the Offerings, 159.

11. "Proper of Time," Solemnities of the Lord during Ordinary Time, The Most Holy Trinity, Collect, 495; "Votive Masses," 1. The Most Holy Trinity, Collect, 1327.

12. "Ritual Masses," I. For the Conferral of the Sacraments of Christian Initiation, 4. For the Conferral of Confirmation, A, Prayer over the Offerings, 1130.

13. "Ritual Masses," X. For the Dedication of a Church and an Altar, 2. For the Dedication of an Altar, Prayer over the Offerings, 1229.

14. Ibid., VI. For the Blessing of an Abbot or an Abbess, 1, For the Blessing of an Abbot, Solemn Blessing, 1199.

one is unity; there is a wholeness or completeness that is formed when Spirit connects to spirit.

This communal unity is expressed throughout the RM. The Mass itself begins with the minister's wish that the communion of the Holy Spirit will be with all gathered together.[15] Every Eucharistic Prayer and major blessing ends with the statement about Christ and the Father being in the unity of the Spirit.[16] Every one of the hundreds of Collects in the RM expresses the living and reigning of Father and Son in the unity of the Holy Spirit. We pray that we may be gathered into unity or into one body by the same Spirit.[17] This is best expressed by the prayer after the first reading on the Vigil of Pentecost; we pray that we will remain God's holy people formed as one by the unity of the Father, the Son, and the Holy Spirit.[18] The unity of the persons of the Trinity of one substance and the equality of their glory[19] is the model for all people united to Christ.[20] The Holy Spirit, who is described as the bond of love between the Father and the Son, is asked to unite in love all peoples of all nations[21] even while such people grow together in unity through the Spirit.[22] The same Spirit brings about the communion of spirit of husband and wife.[23] The OC echoes the RM when it states that the Spirit gathers us in unity of faith and diversity of callings in order to make the church holy and one and to build the body of Christ in unity and love.[24] Spiritual unity, the

---

15. "Order of Mass," par. 2.

16. Ibid., pars. 98, 106, 114, 123; "Appendix," Eucharistic Prayers for Reconciliation, I, par. 8; II, par. 8; Eucharistic Prayer for Use in Masses for Various Needs, I, par. 8; II, par. 8; III, par. 8; IV, par. 8; "Thursday of the Lord's Supper: At the Evening Mass," par. 32; "Easter Sunday," pars. 44, 46.

17. "Order of Mass," pars. 105, 122; "Proper of Time," Easter Time, Wednesday of the Seventh Week of Easter, Collect, 441; "Proper of Saints," The Presentation of the Lord, February 2, par. 4; "Masses and Prayers," I. For Holy Church, 1. For the Church, E, Collect, 1242.

18. "Pentecost Sunday," At the Vigil Mass, Extended Form, par. 5; "Masses and Prayers," I. For Holy Church, 1. For the Church, C, Collect, 1239.

19. "Proper of Time," The Solemnities of the Lord During Ordinary Time, The Most Holy Trinity, Preface, 496–498; "Votive Masses," 1. The Most Holy Trinity, Preface, 1328.

20. "Pentecost Sunday," At the Mass during the Day, Preface, 454–456.

21. "Proper of Saints," Independence Day, July 4, Solemn Blessing, 898.

22. "Masses and Prayers," I. For Holy Church, 1. For the Church, B, Collect, 1238.

23. Ibid., I. For Holy Church, 11. On the Anniversaries of Marriage, B, Collect, 1260.

24. OC, pars. 22, 39, 30, 47.

gathering together of spirits, results in a communion, a wholeness, or completeness that can only be experienced before one writes about it.

Journal/Meditation: When have you recently experienced the communion, wholeness, or completeness brought about by Spirit united to spirits?

Prayer: Heavenly Father, with your Son, Jesus Christ, you live in the unity of the Holy Spirit. Form all people in the same bond of love that you share as a Trinity of persons. Bring me into that solemn communion today, tomorrow, and forever. Amen.

Willing Spirit

Scripture: "Restore to me the joy of your salvation [, O God], and sustain in me a willing spirit." (Ps 51:12)

Reflection: A willing Spirit or spirit is one who is ready to do something without being forced. Such voluntary cooperation is illustrated in the HB (OT) book of Exodus. The narrator states, "... [A]ll the congregation of the Israelites ... came, everyone whose heart was stirred, and everyone whose spirit was willing, and brought the LORD's offering to be used for the tent of meeting, and for all its service, and for the sacred vestments" (Exod 35:20–21). It is found again in the OT (A) Second Book of Maccabees. "May [God] give you all a heart to worship him and to do his will with a strong heart and willing spirit," begins the letter from the Jews in Jerusalem to their Jewish kindred in Egypt (2 Macc 1:3). In the CB (NT), even Jesus acknowledges that "the spirit [of his disciples] indeed is willing, but the flesh is weak" (Mark 14:38; Matt 26:41). Spirit requires a willing spirit in order to connect to spirit, and spirit requires a willing Spirit in order to delve deeper and deeper into spirituality. In the RM, we pray for a generous heart and a willing spirit.[25]

Paul describes having a willing Spirit and having a willing spirit as walking "according to the Spirit" (Rom 8:4), living "according to the Spirit," and setting "minds on the things of the Spirit" (Rom 8:5) which results in life and peace (Rom 8:6). In his Letter to the Galatians, the apostle says, "If we live by the Spirit, let us also be guided by the Spirit" (Gal 5:25). In his First Letter to the Thessalonians, he hopes that the spirit of the Thessalonians will be kept sound, which is another way of wishing them

---

25. "Ritual Masses," I. For the Conferral of the Sacraments of Christian Initiation, 3. For the Conferral of Baptism, A, Eucharistic Prayer II Intercessions, 1127.

a willing spirit (1 Thess 5:23). The spiritual willingness of the Corinthians leads Paul to write to them: "You yourselves are our letter, written on our hearts, to be known and read by all; and you show that you are a letter of Christ, prepared by us, written not with ink but with the Spirit of the living God, not on tablets of stone but on tablets of human hearts" (2 Cor 3:2–3). In other words, the Corinthians are a letter of recommendation, witnesses before the world.[26]

Journal/Meditation: In what specific ways is your spirit willing? How do you experience the willing Spirit? To what witness has your voluntary-cooperative spirit with Spirit led?

Prayer: Sustain in me a willing spirit, O God, that my spirit may voluntarily cooperate with your Spirit. Make me a letter of your Son, Jesus Christ, written not with ink but with your Spirit, giving witness to your presence in the world. You are one God forever and ever. Amen.

Prayer in the Spirit

Scripture: ". . . [Y]ou, beloved, build yourselves up on your most holy faith; pray in the Holy Spirit." (Jude 1:20)

Reflection: The verse above from the Letter of Jude is one of only twenty-five verses of this single-chapter, general letter. The author exhorts his readers to pray in the power of the Spirit. Prayer, best understood as listening to God, is the act of opening the individual spirit to the Spirit and, as best as possible, discerning God's will. This process requires lots of listening; many people think that prayer is telling God what to do, but it is more about God telling us what we need to do. In his Letter to the Romans, Paul states: ". . . [T]he Spirit helps us in our weakness; for we do not know how to pray as we ought, but that very Spirit intercedes with sighs too deep for words. And God, who searches the heart, knows what is the mind of the Spirit, because the Spirit intercedes for the saints according to the will of God" (Rom 8:26–27). In his First Letter to the Corinthians, he states that his spirit prays, that he prays with the spirit, that he sings praise with the spirit, and that he blesses with the spirit (1 Cor 14:14–16). Following the advice of Paul, the author of the Letter to the Ephesians tells his readers, "Pray in the Spirit at all times in every

---

26. "Pentecost Sunday," At the Vigil Mass, par. 8; "Ritual Masses," I. For the Conferral of the Sacraments of Christian Initiation. 4. For the Conferral of Confirmation, A, Prayer over the Offerings, 1130; OC, Collect, Prayer over the Offerings, par. 58.

prayer and supplication" (Eph 6:18a). Thus, when spirit is connected to Spirit, not only are our weak supplications brought to God by the Spirit, but the Spirit brings God's will back to us.

The word of the LORD speaks to the prophet Haggai, telling him, "My spirit abides among you; do not fear" (Hag 2:5b); abiding is another way of writing about prayer in the Spirit. For Haggai, this dwelling among, living among, or residing with leads the author of the First Letter of John to declare that we know that Jesus Christ abides in us "by the Spirit that he has given us" (1 John 3:24). Later, in the same letter, the author writes, "By this we know that we abide in him and he in us, because he has given us of his Spirit" (1 John 4:13). Through Spirit connected to spirit, Christ simultaneously with the Spirit abides in believers. This why every prayer in the RM is presented to the Father, through the Son, in the Holy Spirit.[27] Every time we pray, our spirits pray in the Spirit, who intercedes with God for us; the Son is our mediator, while the Spirit is our lifeline. By persevering in prayer and trusting that the Spirit abides among us,[28] our spirits are in the Spirit and, simultaneously, in Christ.

Journal/Meditation: When have you experienced your spirit praying in the Spirit with sighs too deep for words? How have you experienced the Spirit abiding with you?

Prayer: Father, your Spirit helps people in their weakness; they do not know how to pray as they ought, but your very Spirit intercedes with sighs too deep for words. This day I offer this prayer of praise in the Spirit, who with you and your Son, Jesus Christ, are one God forever and ever. Amen.

Spiritual Blessing

Scripture: ". . . [I]f you say a blessing with the spirit, how can anyone in the position of an outsider say the 'Amen' to your thanksgiving, since the outsider does not know what you are saying?" (1 Cor 14:16)

Reflection: In his First Letter to the Corinthians, Paul identifies himself as a person who speaks in tongues (1 Cor 14:18), but he cautions his readers, ". . . [T]hose who speak in a tongue do not speak to other

---

27. "General Instruction," par. 54.

28. "Pentecost Sunday," At the Vigil Mass, Extended Form, par. 3; "Ritual Masses," I. For the Conferral of the Sacraments of Christian Initiation, 4. For the Conferral of Confirmation, A, Solemn Blessing, 1132; OC, pars. 33, 49.

people but to God; for nobody understands them, since they are speaking mysteries in the Spirit" (1 Cor 14:2). Paul presumes that speaking in a tongue benefits only the individual. That is why he asks in the above verse how can saying a blessing with the spirit in a tongue elicit the appropriate "Amen" from everyone gathered together for prayerful worship because the person blessing cannot be understood. Our focus here is not speaking in a tongue but blessing with the Spirit. Paul states that saying a blessing with the spirit in a tongue not understandable to those present does not get the appropriate "Amen;" no one understands the blessing.

Almost every Mass ends with asking God—Father, Son, and Holy Spirit—to bless the assembly. Sometimes the minister says: "May almighty God bless you, the Father, and the Son, and the Holy Spirit,"[29] and at other times he says: "And may the blessing of almighty God, the Father, and the Son, and the Holy Spirit, come down on you and remain with you forever."[30] In either case, the assembly answers "Amen." We also ask God to look at the offerings of bread and wine and fill them with the blessing of the Holy Spirit.[31] When we bless, we invoke God's help. When blessing with the Spirit, we wish the Spirit to connect to spirits and to elicit and express thanksgiving to God with a hearty "Amen."

Journal/Meditation: When have you experienced the blessing of the Spirit? What thanksgiving to God did you make?

Prayer: Almighty God, you bless people with each of the persons of your Trinity. Grant that the Father bless me with love, that the Son bless me with faith, and that the Spirit bless me with hope today, tomorrow, and forever. Amen.

---

29. "Order of Mass," pars. 141, 143; OC, pars. 33, 49.

30. "Blessings," 674–689; "Easter Sunday," par. 68.

31. "Common of Martyrs," II. During Easter Time, 2, Prayer over the Offerings, 1064.

6

Water and Spirit

Baptism in the Spirit

Scripture: John the Baptizer said, "I have baptized you with water; but [the one more powerful than I who is coming after me] will baptize you with the Holy Spirit." (Mark 1:8)

Reflection: In the oldest account of John the Baptist's preaching—found in Mark's Gospel (70 CE)—he announces a baptism of repentance for the forgiveness of sins, while also making clear that his role is to prepare the way for the One who is more powerful. That One, whom Mark identifies as Jesus of Nazareth, will baptize in the Holy Spirit, just like John baptized in water. The author of Matthew's Gospel (80 CE) and the author of Luke's Gospel (90 CE), who share a source different from Mark—commonly called Q, for *Quelle*, a German word meaning *source*—enlarge the role of the Baptizer. In Matthew's Gospel, John states, "I baptize you with water for repentance, but one who is more powerful than I is coming after me . . . . He will baptize you with the Holy Spirit and fire" (Matt 3:11). Jesus does not fulfill the Baptizer's words in Matthew's Gospel. In Luke's Gospel, John states, "I baptize you with water; but one who is more powerful than I is coming . . . . He will baptize you with the Holy Spirit and fire" (Luke 3:16). The Lukan Jesus fulfills the Baptist's words in the Acts of the Apostles with the event known as Pentecost (Acts 1:5; 2:1–4; 8:16–17; 11:16). The Johannine John the Baptist explains, "... I came baptizing with water for this reason, that he might be revealed to Israel.... [T]he one who sent me to baptize with water said to me, 'He ... is the one who baptizes with the Holy Spirit" (John 1:31, 33). In John's Gospel, Christ returns from the dead and breathes the Spirit on his disciples (John 20:22) in order to fulfill the Baptizer's words.

The Greek word translated *with*—as in *with* the Holy Spirit—can also be translated as *in*—as *in* the Holy Spirit. Thus, John baptizes in water in Mark, Matthew, Luke, and John, but the more powerful one coming after him baptizes in the Holy Spirit. Contrary to the pouring or sprinkling with water that comprises many baptisms today, the Greek verb translated *baptize* means *to immerse* or *to dunk* in water. If we transfer the metaphor to the Spirit, then Jesus immerses or dunks people into the Spirit. Individual spirits are submerged into Spirit. In Paul's First Letter to the Corinthians, he writes, "... [I]n the one Spirit we were all baptized into one body—Jews or Greeks, slaves or free..." (1 Cor 12:13). Spiritual (Spirit) energy seeks human spiritual (spirit) energy in order to draw human spiritual (spirit) energy into its divine self. Human spirit is immersed, surrounded, submerged in Spirit and transformed into it.

Journal/Meditation: When have you experienced being baptized—immersed, surrounded, or submerged—in Spirit? What transformation took place in you?

Prayer: Your servant John the Baptizer announced the coming of your Son, O LORD, in order to bathe the world in your Holy Spirit. Continue to transform my spirit with your Spirit, who lives and reigns with you and Jesus Christ, one God, forever and ever. Amen.

Water and Dove

Scripture: "... [J]ust as [Jesus] was coming up out of the water, he saw the heavens torn apart and the Spirit descending like a dove on him." (Mark 1:11)

Reflection: The author of Mark's Gospel narrates that after Jesus is immersed in the Jordan River by John the Baptist, he comes up out of the water to see the heavens torn apart and, like a dove, the Spirit descends upon him. The author of Matthew's Gospel enlarges and literalizes the narrative, writing, "And when Jesus had been baptized, just as he came up from the water, suddenly the heavens were opened to him and he saw the Spirit of God descending like a dove and alighting on him"

(Matt 3:16). The author of Luke's Gospel states, ". . . [T]he heaven was opened, and the Holy Spirit descended upon [Jesus] in bodily form like a dove" (Luke 3:21–22a). In the Acts of the Apostles, Luke will portray Peter interpreting this event as God's anointing of Jesus with the Holy Spirit (Acts 10:38). In John's Gospel, John the Baptist testifies, "I saw the Spirit descending from heaven like a dove, and it remained on [Jesus].... [T]he one who sent me to baptize with water said to me, 'He on whom you see the Spirit descend and remain is the one who baptizes with the Holy Spirit'" (John 1:32–33).

All these texts presume a world that is composed of three levels. Above the heavens, level one, is where God lives. Below the heavens on the earth, level two, is where people live. And below the earth, level three, is where the dead live! In order to demonstrate that Jesus is the chosen or anointed one of God (*Messiah* in Hebrew; *Christ* in Greek), the evangelists portray the heavens either being torn apart or opened in order to portray God as Spirit, like a dove, descending upon Jesus. The dove is the chosen metaphor for Spirit because it echoes the great flood story in the HB (OT) book of Genesis. "At the end of the flood, whose symbolism refers to baptism," states the CCC, "a dove released by Noah returns with a fresh olive-tree branch in its beak as a sign that the earth was again habitable"[1] (Gen 8:8–12). Just as the dove indicates the habitability of the earth in Genesis, so does the dove indicate the habitability of Spirit in Jesus in the synoptic (Mark, Matthew, Luke) gospels. The RM refers to the Spirit descending upon Jesus in the likeness of a dove.[2] Furthermore, the metaphor of dove for Spirit indicates its innocence (Matt 10:16). All this is brought together in Matthew's great commissioning narrative, where Jesus tells his disciples to baptize in the name of the Holy Spirit (Matt 28:19). The OC interprets Jesus' baptism as his anointing with the Spirit and his sending forth for his ministry of setting the earth on fire with the Spirit.[3]

Journal/Meditation: What other reflection does the Spirit-like-a-dove metaphor spark in you? How do you experience yourself (your spirit) being the habitat for Spirit?

Prayer: When John the Baptist immersed your Son, Jesus Christ, in the Jordan River, Father, the heavens opened and the Spirit alighted on

---

1. CCC, par. 701.
2. "Proper of Time," Baptism of the Lord, Collect, Preface, 202, 204–205.
3. OC, pars. 22, 39.

him like a dove. Make of me a worthy habitat for you with your Son in the unity of the Holy Spirit now and forever. Amen.

Born of Water and Spirit

Scripture: Jesus said, "Very truly, I tell you, no one can enter the kingdom of God without being born of water and Spirit." (John 3:5)

Reflection: The verse above from John's Gospel is one of Jesus' pronouncements in his dialogue with the unique Johannine character named Nicodemus. Only in this verse and in verse 3 before it does Jesus speak about the kingdom of God in John's Gospel. ". . . [N]o one can see the kingdom of God without being born from above," states Jesus (John 3:3). To be born anew is to be born of water; to be born from above is to be born of Spirit. ". . . [W]hat is born of the Spirit is spirit," states the Johannine Jesus (John 1:6). Later, he will add that rivers of living water will flow out of the hearts of believers (John 7:38); the narrator interprets this: "Now he said this about the Spirit, which believers in him were to receive; for as yet there was no Spirit, because Jesus was not yet glorified" (John 7:39). Paul tells the Romans that they have received a spirit of adoption through baptism (Rom 8:15). For Paul, baptism is a reenactment of Jesus death and resurrection. A person is baptized into his death and is buried with him; then the person is raised to new life with him (Rom 6:3–11). In other words, the person is born again as an adopted child of God, and the Spirit bears witness with his or her spirit that he or she is a child of God (Rom 8:16). He or she has been born according to the Spirit (Gal 4:29). The Pauline author of the Letter to Titus explains: ". . . [W]hen the goodness and loving kindness of God our Savior appeared, he saved us, not because of any works of righteousness that we had done, but according to his mercy, through the water of rebirth and renewal by the Holy Spirit" (Titus 3:5).

According to the CCC, water signifies the action of the Spirit. During the Easter Vigil, God is asked to infuse the water for baptism with the Spirit.[4] Thus, those who are immersed in the font are given a new birth

---

4. "Easter Sunday," pars. 44, 46.

of water and the Holy Spirit;[5] they are declared to be reborn,[6] reborn in the Spirit,[7] or reborn from water and the Spirit.[8] They have experienced the cleansing waters of rebirth and the gift of the Spirit.[9] They have been brought to new birth by water and the Spirit.[10] On the Second Sunday of Easter, we pray that we might grasp and rightly understand in what font we have been washed and by whose Spirit we have been reborn.[11] ". . . [J]ust as the gestation of our first birth took place in water," states the CCC, "so the water of baptism truly signifies that our birth into the divine life is given to us in the Holy Spirit."[12]

Journal/Meditation: Since we do not remember being born, how can receiving the Spirit be like being born again? For you what kind of renewal is like being reborn?

Prayer: Through water and your Spirit, O God, you give people new birth. Help me to grasp and to rightly understand in what font I have been washed and by whose Spirit I have been reborn. I ask this in the name of Jesus, who is Lord forever and ever. Amen.

Water and Wind

Scripture: "In the beginning when God created the heavens and the earth, the earth was a formless void and darkness covered the face of the deep, while a wind from God swept over the face of the waters." (Gen 1:1–2)

Reflection: Because the Hebrew word *ruach* can mean breath, air, wind, or spirit, the first two verses from the HB (OT) book of Genesis

---

5. "Order of Mass," par. 87; "Easter Sunday," par. 55; "Ritual Masses," I. For the Conferral of the Sacraments of Christian Initiation, 3. For the Conferral of Baptism, A, Eucharist Prayer I Commemoration, 1127.

6. "Proper of Time," Easter Time, Tuesday of the Third Week of Easter, Collect, 406.

7. "Proper of Saints," Independence Day, July 4, Preface II, 896–897.

8. "Ritual Masses," I. For the Conferral of the Sacraments of Christian Initiation, 4. For the Conferral of Confirmation, A, Solemn Blessing, 1132; OC, pars. 25, 33, 42, 49, 54.

9. Ibid., 3. For the Conferral of Baptism, A, Eucharist Prayer III Commemoration, 1128.

10. Ibid., Eucharist Prayer IV Commemoration, 1128.

11. "Proper of Time," Easter Time, Second Sunday of Easter, Collect, 395; "Votive Masses," 2. The Mercy of God, Collect, 1329.

12. CCC, par. 694.

could also be translated as the breath from God, the air from God, or the spirit from God swept over the waters. Before crossing the Red Sea, the LORD divides its waters with a strong wind (Exod 14:21; 15:10). The prophet Elijah ascends to heaven in a whirlwind (2 Kgs 2:1, 11). The OT (A) book of Sirach states that Elijah was taken up by a whirlwind of fire (Sir 48:9), further making the connection between wind, fire, and Spirit. Likewise, Isaiah declares that the city of Jerusalem will be visited by the LORD with whirlwind and fire (Isa 29:6). Twice we are told in the HB (OT) book of Job that God answers him out of a whirlwind (Job 38:1; 40:6). Ezekiel experiences the LORD in a stormy wind (Ezek 1:4), which is echoed in his narrative about the valley with the dry bones. The LORD says to him, "Prophesy to the breath, prophesy, mortal and say to the breath: Thus says the Lord GOD: Come from the four winds, O breath, and breathe upon these slain, that they may live" (Ezek 37:9). Literally, the word *breath* could also be translated air, wind, or spirit in Ezek 37:9 to tease the ambiguity from the text. The author of the Prayer of Azariah notes that it is the angel of the Lord, in this case a code name for Spirit, who comes into the furnace with the men and makes "the inside of the furnace as though a moist wind were whistling through it" (Sg Three 1:27 [Dan 3:50]).

However, it is in John's Gospel where the merger of water, wind, and Spirit takes place. The Johannine Jesus has explained to the unique Johannine character named Nicodemus that he must be born of water and Spirit (John 3:5). Then, he says, "The wind blows where it chooses, and you hear the sound of it, but you do not know where it comes from or where it goes. So it is with everyone who is born of the Spirit" (John 3:8). Just as one cannot "restrain the wind" (Prov 27:16), so one cannot control the Spirit. Thus, the author of the Acts of the Apostles writes about the "sound like the rush of a violent wind" (Acts 2:2) from heaven on Pentecost that fills the entire house where the apostles are staying, and all of them are filled with the Spirit (Acts 2:4). Just like the windy Spirit swept over water before creation and divided water for the exodus; just like Elijah ascend to heaven in a Spirit-whirlwind and God visits Jerusalem and Job in the same; just like the windy-Spirit reanimates dry bones and cools the inside of a raging furnace, so does the violent wind of Pentecost fill disciples with the Spirit. The wind cannot be captured, contained, or harnessed; it can only be experienced. Such is the Spirit.

Journal/Meditation: In what specific ways have you experienced the Spirit being like the wind? Which Scripture passage mentioned above best helps you to interpret your experience?

Prayer: Come, Holy Spirit, like a mighty wind, into my life. Grant that every breath of air I take may be of the divine life you share with the Father and his Son, Jesus Christ, today, tomorrow, and forever. Amen.

New Spirit

Scripture: Thus says the Lord GOD: "I will give [Israel] one heart, and put a new spirit within them; I will remove the heart of stone from their flesh and give them a heart of flesh." (Ezek 11:19)

Reflection: In terms of "a new spirit"—or breath, air, or wind—that God will put in the Israelites (Jews) in Babylonian captivity, the prophet Ezekiel has a monopoly. Later, Ezekiel records the Lord GOD telling the Jews, "Cast away from you all the transgressions that you have committed against me, and get yourselves a new heart and a new spirit!" (Ezek 18:31a) Again, the Lord GOD says to the house of Israel: "A new heart I will give you, and a new spirit I will put within you; and I will remove from your body the heart of stone and give you a heart of flesh. I will put my spirit within you . . ." (Ezek 36:26–27). The prophet Jeremiah records God saying that he will give his people a new heart (Jer 31:31–34; 32:36–41), but it is Ezekiel who records the LORD giving them a new spirit. Ezekiel's words echo a verse of Psalm 51: "Create in me a clean heart, O God, and put a new and right spirit within me" (Ps 51:10). The steadfast spirit sought by the psalmist is expressed in the OT (A) book of Wisdom as knowing who formed one, inspired one with active souls, and breathed a living spirit into one (Wis 15:11).

In the CB (NT), the new Spirit of Ezekiel becomes Paul's "new life of the Spirit" (Rom 7:6). According to Paul, we have been discharged from the law (Rom 7:6) through Christ Jesus' death and resurrection: "For the law of the Spirit of life in Christ Jesus has set [us] free from the law of sin and of death" (Rom 8:2). In his Second Letter to the Corinthians, the apostle adds that now we live not according to the letter of the law, but according to the spirit; "for the letter kills, but the Spirit gives life" (2 Cor 3:6). For Paul, letter represents the six hundred thirteen precepts of Torah; Spirit represents the life-giving resurrection of Christ Jesus from the dead. In other words, Spirit transforms stony spirit-hearts into new

Spirit-hearts. The ordinary human spirit-heart is a dwelling place for Spirit.

Journal/Meditation: What stony-heart spiritual transformation has been wrought in you by the Spirit? What new life have you experienced as a result of the transformation?

Prayer: I know you formed me, O LORD, inspired me with an active soul, and breathed a living spirit into me. Create in me a clean heart, and put a new and right spirit within me. I ask this through my Lord Jesus Christ, who died and rose in order to give me new life in the Spirit now and forever. Amen.

Refreshed Spirit

Scripture: "Like the cold of snow in the time of harvest are faithful messengers to those who send them; they refresh the spirit of their masters." (Prov 25:13)

Reflection: Another result of Spirit connecting to spirit is refreshment. This is illustrated in the HB (OT) book of Proverbs. The refreshed spirit of masters occurs because the messengers they send deliver the messages faithfully. It is important to keep in mind here that these are not necessarily written messages (or texts or e-mails); they are memorized messages. The masters' refreshment of spirit is like the cold of snow in the time of harvest. This is not a destructive snowstorm during harvest, but snow from the past winter gathered from the mountains and stored—like blocks of ice cut from a river and stored in an ice house through the spring and summer—that was put in drinks (water, wine, etc.) to cool them before giving them to the harvesters to consume. In other words, the refreshment brought by a snow cone is like a business man's spirit refreshed by his courier faithfully and timely delivering important documents. The proverb has been garnered from ancient real-life experiences of refreshed spirits. For example, when Jacob hears that his son, Joseph, is still alive, his spirit is revived (Gen 45:27). After Samson drinks water from a hollow place split open by God, "his spirit returned, and he revived" (Judg 15:19). David drinks water and eats bread, fig cake, and raisins, after having nothing to eat for three days, and his spirit revives (1 Sam 30:11–12). The prophet Isaiah summarizes all this, when he records God's words: "For thus says the high and lofty one who inhabits eternity, whose name is Holy: I dwell in the high and holy place, and also with those who are contrite and humble in spirit, to revive the spirit of the humble, and to revive the heart of the contrite" (Isa 57:15).

In the CB (NT), Paul tells the Corinthians that he was made happy by the arrival of three men, who refreshed his spirit (1 Cor 16:18). The Pauline author of the Letter to the Ephesians reminds the readers that they were taught to put away their former way of life "and to be renewed in the spirit of [their] minds" (Eph 4:23). This latter concept is found in the RM. On Easter Sunday, we ask God for renewal brought by the Spirit.[13] Likewise, on the Third Sunday of Easter and during the Pentecost Vigil, we rejoice in the renewed youthfulness of spirit.[14] Thus, no matter if one's spirit is refreshed, revived, or renewed by the Spirit, he or she is left with a youthfulness that is the result of Spirit connected to spirit.

Journal/Meditation: When has your spirit been most recently refreshed, revived, or renewed by the Spirit? What youthfulness did you experience as a result?

Prayer: High and lofty God, whose name is Holy, you inhabit eternity. You dwell in the high and holy place, and you send the Spirit to refresh, revive, and renew those who are contrite and humble in spirit. Refresh, revive, and renew my spirit with your Holy Spirit. I ask this in the name of your Son, Jesus Christ, now and forever. Amen.

Spiritual Transformation

Scripture: ". . . [A]ll of us, with unveiled faces, seeing the glory of the Lord as though reflected in a mirror, are being transformed into the same image from one degree of glory to another; for this comes from the Lord, the Spirit." (2 Cor 3:18)

Reflection: Another result of Spirit connected to spirit is illustrated by Paul in his Second Letter to the Corinthians. Paul says that through the death and resurrection of Christ Jesus, we are now able to see the glory—or the brightness—of God. In the past, a person could not look on God and live. Now, with unveiled faces, we see God's glory in the person of the risen Jesus, even though it is like seeing our reflection in a mirror. In other words, Jesus is the mirror into which we look to see God's glory. Furthermore, through the death and resurrection of Jesus, we are

---

13. "Easter Sunday," par. 72.

14. "Proper of Time," Easter Time, Third Sunday of Easter, Collect, 403; "Pentecost Sunday," At the Vigil Mass, Extended form, par. 7.

transformed by God's glory into glory a little at a time, and this is made possible by the Spirit. When Spirit inhabits spirit, we become more glorified step by step. The change is subtle; it does not always occur immediately as when God changes the spirit of King Artaxerxes from anger to gentleness (Add Esth 15:8 [D:8]), and Queen Esther is welcomed into his presence. In the OT (A) book of Esther, the king's spirit is transformed by God through the queen, who takes her life in her hands by approaching him without being summoned.

The Spirit is the Lord, according to Paul, the giver of life and the transformer of spirit. In the RM, we pray for transformation of our spirit by the Spirit. We ask God to give us a Christian spirit to do what we need to do;[15] to fill us with the spirit of divine sonship, daughtership, or adoption;[16] and, after being transformed over and over again, we ask God, finally, to raise us through the Holy Spirit to eternal life.[17] Glorification will be finalized only through death, just like it was for Jesus. It is after his death that the Spirit raised his spirit to new life, that is, glorified him. We await the last step in our spiritual glorification process.

Journal/Meditation: What transformation has occurred in you because your spirit was connected to Spirit? What were you inspired to do?

Prayer: Ever-living God, you have revealed your glory through the death and resurrection of your Son, Jesus Christ. As you transform my spirit from one degree to glory to another with your Spirit, grant that I may willing do what you inspire until the day I am transfigured by the Spirit into eternal life. I ask this through Christ my Lord. Amen.

Different Spirit

Scripture: The LORD said, ". . . [M]y servant Caleb, because he has a different spirit and has followed me wholeheartedly, I will bring into the land into which he went, and his descendants shall possess it." (Num 14:24)

Reflection: Because of the grumbling of the Israelites in the wilderness, Moses intercedes with the LORD for them. He forgives them, but refuses to let any of them enter the promised land because they have not

---

15. "Masses and Prayers," II. For Civil Needs, 26. For the Sanctification of Human Labor, B, Collect, 1291.

16. Ibid., 29. For the Progress of Peoples, Prayer over the Offerings, 1296.

17. "Proper of Saints," St. Polycarp, February 23, Collect, 829.

obeyed him (Num 14:1–38). At first it is only Caleb, son of Jephunneh, who is granted access to the promised land because his spirit of faithfulness is different from all the other Israelites, but then later the LORD permits Joshua, son of Nun, to enter (Num 14:30). Earlier in the HB (OT) book of Numbers, Caleb, one of the men sent to spy the land of Canaan, had quieted the people before Moses, saying, "Let us go up at once and occupy it, for we are well able to overcome it" (Num 13:30). However, the rest of the men sent with Caleb strongly disagree with him, and this causes the Israelites to complain. Caleb possesses a spirit that differs from all the other Israelites. In his spirit there is no deceit (Ps 32:3).

In the account of the complaint of the Israelites in Numbers, the people need to adopt a different spirit. Paul recognizes this in his directions to the Corinthians about how to handle a man living with his father's wife; he is to be dismissed from the community "so that his spirit may be saved in the day of the Lord" (1 Cor 5:5). He also criticizes the Corinthians for their wish-washy faith, submitting to what someone other than Paul preaches to them. They are led astray by receiving a different spirit from the one they received when Paul preached Christ to them (2 Cor 11:4). He also criticizes them for their failure to recognize that he conducted himself with the same spirit as others who did not take advantage of the Corinthians (2 Cor 12:18). In the RM, we acknowledge that we need to turn back to God in spirit[18] to let the coming of the Spirit cleanse our consciences,[19] because the Spirit is the remission of all sins.[20]

Journal/Meditation: How is your spirit like Caleb's? What turning in spirit to God do you need to do?

Prayer: Your servant Caleb followed you wholeheartedly, O LORD, because his spirit was directed by your Spirit. See me turning back to you in spirit, and fill me with the Spirit of faithfulness. I ask this in the name of your Son, Jesus Christ, who lives and reigns with you and the Holy Spirit, one God, forever and ever. Amen.

---

18. "Appendix," Eucharistic Prayers for Reconciliation, I, par. 1.

19. "Proper of Time," Easter Time, Friday of the Seventh Week of Easter, Prayer over the Offerings, 443.

20. Ibid., Saturday of the Seventh Week of Easter, At the Morning Mass, Prayer over the Offerings, 444.

7

Led by the Spirit

Guided by Spirit

Scripture: "Each [of the four living creatures] moved straight ahead; wherever the spirit would go, they went, without turning as they went." (Ezek 1:12)

Reflection: In the first of the prophet Ezekiel's many visions, he describes four living creatures, each with four faces—human, lion, ox, eagle—four wings, and sparkling like burnished bronze. While the vision is interesting (Ezek 1:4–28a), our concern here is the guidance given divine intelligence (human), royalty (lion), strength (ox), and mobility (eagle) by the Spirit. According to the prophet, "Wherever the spirit would go, they went, and the wheels rose along with them; for the spirit of the living creatures was in the wheels" (Ezek 1:20, 21; 10:17). In other words, God is in constant motion in all four directions on the earth; this is another way of saying that the earth is the home of divine presence. In the CB (NT), the author of Luke's Gospel and the Acts of the Apostles presents Simeon, who is guided by the Spirit (Luke 2:27), and Paul, who resolves in the Spirit to go on the next leg of his journey (Acts 19:21). In his letter to the Romans, Paul declares, ". . . [A]ll who are led by the Spirit of God are children of God" (Rom 8:14), while in his Letter to the Galatians, he writes that those who are led by the Spirit are no longer subject to the law

(Gal 5:18). He concludes: "If we live by the Spirit, let us also be guided by the Spirit" (Gal 5:25).

In the RM, we pray to be faithful to the promptings of the Spirit,[1] like Simeon and Anna were prompted by the Spirit to go to the Temple when Joseph and Mary brought Jesus there.[2] We also ask for the Spirit to lead us to all truth,[3] because we are governed by the Spirit.[4] The author of the Letter to the Hebrews attributes the Spirit with indicating that before Christ the way into the heavenly sanctuary had not yet been disclosed (Heb 9:8). However, once Christ came as high priest and offered himself to God through the Spirit, access was gained to the heavenly sanctuary (Heb 9:11–14). In order for the Spirit to lead, there must be spirit to follow. That is why we pay attention in our spirit to the promptings of the Spirit.

Journal/Meditation: What has the Spirit prompted your spirit to do? To whom or what or where did the Spirit lead your spirit?

Prayer: Heavenly God, you guided Simeon, Anna, and Paul with the Holy Spirit. Lead me with your Spirit that I may be your child in deed and in fact. Help me to live by the promptings of the Spirit until I reach the sanctuary where you live and reign as one God—Father, Son, and Holy Spirit—forever and ever. Amen.

David Led by Spirit

Scripture: ". . . Samuel took the horn of oil, and anointed [David] in the presence of his brothers; and the spirit of the LORD came mightily upon David from that day forward." (1 Sam 16:13a)

Reflection: Not only does the narrator of the First Book of Samuel declare that the Spirit came mightily upon King David to lead him, but the Second Book of Samuel records some of his last words as: "The spirit of the LORD speaks through me, his word is upon my tongue" (2 Sam 23:2). In the CB (NT), while teaching in the Temple, the Markan Jesus asks, "How can the scribes say that the Messiah is the son of David? David

---

1. "Proper of Saints," Visitation of the Blessed Virgin Mary, May 31, Collect, 867.

2. Ibid., Presentation of the Lord, Blessing of Candles and the Procession, February 2, par. 4.

3. Ibid., St. Anthony Zaccaria, July 5, Collect, 899; "Votive Masses," 9. The Holy Spirit, B, Collect, 1341; OC, par. 60.

4. "Votive Masses," 9. The Holy Spirit, C, Collect, 1344.

himself, by the Holy Spirit, declared, 'The Lord said to my Lord, "Sit at my right hand, until I put your enemies under your feet."' David himself calls him Lord; so how can he be his son?" (Mark 12:35–37a) When the author of Matthew's Gospel reads this passage, he changes the audience to Pharisees, and Jesus asks them: "'What do you think of the Messiah? Whose son is he?' They said to him, 'The son of David.' He said to them 'How is it then that David by the Spirit calls him Lord, saying, "The Lord said to my Lord, 'Sit at my right hand, until I put your enemies under your feet'"? If David thus calls him Lord, how can he be his son?'" (Matt 22:42–45) When the author of Luke's Gospel reads his Markan source, he removes any mention of the Spirit (Luke 20:41–44). However, in Luke's second volume, the Acts of the Apostles, Peter declares that the Holy Spirit foretold Judas's fate through David (Acts 1:16), and, in a prayer, all the disciples declare that by the Holy Spirit through David, God had predicted the fate of Jesus (Acts 4:25–26).

The authors of the CB (NT) presumed that David was led by the Spirit and inspired to write Psalms 2, 69, 109, and 110. The author of Mark's Gospel presents Jesus quoting the David-inspired Psalm 110, the most quoted psalm in the Bible. The author of Matthew's Gospel and Luke's Gospel follow their Markan source, although Luke removes the reference to David as the inspired author of Psalm 110. In the Acts of the Apostles, Peter quotes from Psalms 69 and 109, stating that the Spirit inspired David to write those psalms. Among these four psalms, 69, 109, and 110 carry the superscription "of David" found immediately below the psalm number in most Bibles and, in the Septuagint (the Greek translation of the HB [OT]), numbered as verse 1. Did David know that he was being inspired to write psalms, if, as some scholars doubt, he actually wrote all those attributed to him? Being led by the Spirit may be an after-the-fact phenomenon; we stop and reflect on an event in our lives or the writing of another and discover inspiration which prompts a change in our behavior and/or words. Who knows? Maybe a day in the future someone will read our written words and be inspired by them.

Journal/Meditation: What have you read recently that inspired you? How was the Spirit leading you? To what did the Spirit lead you?

Prayer: LORD God, once you spoke by the Spirit through your anointed King David, inviting him to set at your right hand of power, while you conquered his enemies. In the fullness of time, you spoke by the Spirit through your Son, Jesus Christ, who conquered his enemies on a cross. Inspire me with the same Spirit that I may serve you all my days. I ask in the name of Jesus now and forever. Amen.

Mary Led by Spirit

Scripture: "The angel [Gabriel] said to [Mary], 'The Holy Spirit will come upon you, and the power of the Most High will overshadow you; therefore the child to be born will be holy; he will be called Son of God.'" (Luke 1:35)

Reflection: The author of Luke's Gospel considers Mary to be overshadowed by the Holy Spirit and God's power, like the cloud of divine presence protected the Israelites from harm and from God's holiness (Exod 19:16; 40:35). The same cloud appears in the transfiguration narrative and speaks to three of Jesus' disciples gathered with him (Mark 9:7; Matt 17:5; Luke 9:34), just as the voice spoke from the cloud on Mount Sinai (Horeb) (Exod 19:9, 21). Furthermore, the risen Jesus tells his apostles, ". . . [Y]ou will receive power when the Holy Spirit has come upon you . . ." (Acts 1:8). Thus, according to the author of Luke's Gospel, Mary's Son is a Spirit-child, whose birth is by divine power, and who, like the angel Gabriel before him, announces the overshadowing power of the Spirit to his apostles. In Matthew's Gospel, Mary "was found to be with child from the Holy Spirit" (Matt 1:18). The angel of the Lord, who appears in a dream to Joseph, Mary's fiancé, tells him "the child conceived in her is from the Holy Spirit" (Matt 1:20). Matthew has in mind the creative spirit (breath, air, or wind) of God sweeping over the face of the waters (Gen 1:2). Thus, the instrument of Jesus' conception and birth is the Spirit in Matthew's Gospel, just as the instrument of the birth of creation is the Spirit in the HB (OT) book of Genesis.

The Scriptural references to Mary being led by the Spirit are incorporated in the RM. The Nicene Creed declares that Jesus was incarnate of the Virgin Mary by the Spirit,[5] while the Apostles' Creed echoes Matthew's Gospel about him being conceived by the Spirit.[6] Luke's Gospel is echoed when we declare that it was by the overshadowing of the Spirit that Mary conceived Jesus.[7] Matthew's Gospel is echoed when we de-

---

5. "Order of Mass," par. 18.

6. Ibid., par. 19.

7. Ibid., par. 62; "Proper of Saints," St. Joseph, Spouse of the Blessed Virgin Mary, March 19, Preface, 836-838; Annunciation of the Lord, March 25, Preface, 842-843;

clare that Jesus was made incarnate by the Spirit and born of the Virgin.[8] In the Prayer over the Offerings on the Fourth Sunday of Advent, we acknowledge that the Holy Spirit filled with his power the womb of Mary.[9] The mother of Jesus is led by the Spirit, manifest as an overshadowing cloud full of divine power. Just as that Spirit overshadowed her, it overshadowed his apostles, and it continues to overshadow us today. The instrument for our inspired ideas, words, or deeds is the same Spirit, who was the instrument for the conception and birth of Jesus in Mary's womb. Just as he filled her with his power, he continues to fill us with his power.

Journal/Meditation: In what specific way—idea, word, or deed—have you been overshadowed by the Holy Spirit? What was the sign of your inspiration?

Prayer: Your Holy Spirit filled the womb of Mary with your power, Father, and she conceived your Son, Jesus Christ. Overshadow me with your Spirit that my ideas, words, and deeds may give you glory now and forever. Amen.

Jesus Led by Spirit

Scripture: "... [T]he Spirit immediately drove [Jesus] out into the wilderness. He was in the wilderness forty days tempted by Satan...." (Mark 1:12–13)

Reflection: In between Mark's account of Jesus' baptism and his forty-day temptation by Satan, there is the above verse about the Spirit, who had descended like a dove on Jesus at his baptism (Mark 1:10), driving him into the wilderness. In Matthew's Gospel, after he is baptized, the author narrates: "Then Jesus was led up by the Spirit into the wilderness to be tempted by the devil" (Matt 4:1). In Luke's Gospel, after Jesus had been baptized by no one (Luke 3:21–22), the author presents a genealogy before narrating: "Jesus, full of the Holy Spirit, returned from the Jordan and was led by the Spirit into the wilderness, where for forty days he was tempted by the devil" (Luke 4:1–2a).

St. Joseph the Worker, May 1, Preface, 855–856; "Votive Masses," 13. St. Joseph, Preface, 1357–1358.

8. "Order of Mass," pars. 77, 99, 117.

9. "Proper of Time," Advent, Fourth Sunday of Advent, Prayer over the Offerings, 159.

In each of the above accounts, Jesus is either driven or led by the Spirit to the wilderness in order to be tempted by either Satan or the devil immediately after his baptism. While it may seem very strange to modern readers that the Spirit leads Jesus to temptation, the point is that baptism does not spare us from trials and testing anymore than it spared Jesus. Mark's account of Jesus' temptation is very short in comparison to the three temptations with dialogue between Jesus and the devil in the Q account found in Matthew and Luke. In his one verse about the Spirit driving Jesus into the wilderness in Mark's Gospel, the author establishes a theme that he will employ throughout his work, namely, that Jesus drives out demons (Mark 1:34, 39; 3:15, 22, 23; 6:13; 7:26; 9:18, 28, 38) with overtones of coercion (Mark 5:40; 9:47; 11:5; 12:8). Furthermore, Mark prefers the Satan, the adversary, who makes his first appearance in the HB (OT) book of Job as a member of God's court (Job 1:6–7). The author of Matthew's Gospel has in mind the testing undergone by the Israelites in the desert (Deut 8:2) to determine their fidelity to the covenant. Like his ancestors, Jesus is led by the Spirit to the devil's test to demonstrate his fidelity as Son of God. In Luke's Gospel, the devil is viewed as the ruler of an opposing kingdom within which demons and unclean spirits exist for Jesus to confront throughout the rest of the narrative. The point of the Spirit driving or leading Jesus to temptation is to demonstrate his overcoming of evil which is narrated throughout each gospel. He is not immune to evil, even as Son of God, but must confront it wherever he finds it. By being driving or led by the Spirit, he demonstrates that evil is no match for him or God.

Journal/Meditation: Have you ever been driven by the Spirit? Explain. Have you ever been led by the Spirit? Explain. What evil did you confront?

Prayer: Almighty God, your Spirit drove your Son, Jesus Christ, into the desert to test his faithfulness to you. When I encounter evil, lead me with your Spirit through the temptation to the kingdom, where you live and reign as one God—Father, Son, and Holy Spirit—forever and ever. Amen.

Spirit Teacher

Scripture: Jesus said: "When they bring you before the synagogues, the rulers, and the authorities, do not worry about how you are to defend yourself or what you are to say; for the Holy Spirit will teach you at that very hour what you ought to say." (Luke 12:11–12)

Reflection: Besides the Lukan Jesus' words about the Spirit teaching the disciples, there is the notation in the Acts of the Apostles about Jesus giving his apostles instructions through the Spirit (Acts 1:2). As an instructor, according to Paul, the Spirit helps us in our weakness, because we do not know how to pray (Rom 8:26; Phil 1:19). The Sprit even knows the mind of God (Rom 8:27). Being such a good teacher, the Spirit can even forbid Paul and Timothy from speaking or going to certain places (Acts 16:6–7). In John's Gospel, it is the Advocate, the Holy Spirit, whom the Father sends in Jesus' name, who teaches everything to Jesus' disciples and reminds them of all he said to them (John 14:26). The Spirit of truth remains in the church today.[10]

This role of teacher for the Spirit originates in the prophets. With tongue in cheek, Hosea presents Israel crying, "The prophet is a fool, the man of the spirit is mad!" (Hos 9:7) Zechariah, too, writes about the Israelites, who "made their hearts adamant in order not to hear the law and the words that the Lord of hosts had sent by his spirit through the former prophets" (Zech 7:12). This is echoed by Nehemiah, who records Ezra saying, "Many years you [, LORD,] were patient with them, and warned them by your spirit through your prophets; yet they would not listen" (Neh 9:30a). In the Acts of the Apostles, Paul addresses the Jews in Rome, stating, "The Holy Spirit was right in saying to your ancestors through the prophet Isaiah, 'Go to this people and say, You will indeed listen, but never understand, and you will indeed look, but never perceive'" (Acts 28:25–26; Isa 6:9). Isaiah records the hostility of the people to his prophetic message—which Paul attributes to the Spirit and applies anew to the Jews—and their refusal to accept it. In biblical understanding, prophecy comes from the Spirit. The Spirit teaches the prophet, who is commissioned by the same Spirit to teach the people to whom the prophet is sent. According to the Lukan Jesus, Spirit transforms a person, moving him or her to speech and action beyond his or her expected capacities. The prophet's words arise from inspiration. In the Creed, we declare that the Spirit has spoken through the prophets.[11]

Journal/Meditation: Specifically, what has the Spirit taught your spirit? Were you inspired? Explain.

---

10. OC, pars. 33, 49.
11. "Order of Mass," par. 18.

Prayer: Father, your Son has taught us not to worry when we may need to defend ourselves, for the Holy Spirit teaches us what we ought to say. Fill me with prophetic inspiration that both my words and deeds bear witness to Jesus Christ, who is Lord forever and ever. Amen.

Spirit of Wisdom

Scripture: "I called on God, and the spirit of wisdom came to me." (Wis 7:7b)

Reflection: The Spirit leads by giving us the gift of wisdom. In the OT (A) book of Wisdom, Solomon speaks autobiographically, declaring that he asked God for wisdom, and "wisdom, the fashioner of all things, taught [him]" (Wis 7:22). The HB (OT) book of Deuteronomy's narrator states that Joshua "was full of the spirit of wisdom, because Moses had laid his hands on him" (Deut 34:9). It is from the prophet Isaiah that we learn about the spirit of the LORD resting on the stump of Jesse—the hoped for Davidic descendant after the Babylonian captivity—and giving him the spirit of wisdom (Isa 11:2). In the CB (NT), the author of the Letter to the Ephesians states, "I pray that the God of our Lord Jesus Christ, the Father of glory, may give you a spirit of wisdom . . ." (Eph 1:17).

The Spirit of Wisdom is a guide which enables us to judge correctly concerning the ways of God. Better known as discernment, wisdom is the good sense required to make reasonable decisions based on information and experience. We see something about God that was not very clear or obvious. That is why we pray in the RM that God will endow with a spirit of wisdom those who govern others,[12] and that he will pour out a spirit of wisdom on a governing assembly.[13] We also ask that in the Spirit we may be truly wise.[14] In the OC, the minister asks God to send upon the candidates the Holy Spirit to give them the spirit of wisdom.[15] With the Spirit of Wisdom as a guide, we can be confident that our decisions are God's will because the Spirit of Wisdom has communicated the divine desires to our spirits.

---

12. "Masses and Prayers," I. For Holy Church, 5. For a Council or a Synod, Collect, 1248.
13. Ibid., II. For Civil Needs, 23. For a Governing Assembly, Collect, 1287.
14. "Votive Masses," 9. The Holy Spirit, A, Collect, 1338.
15. OC, pars. 25, 42, 54.

Journal/Meditation: When have you experienced the Spirit of Wisdom guiding you in the ways of God? Explain.

Prayer: God of our Lord Jesus Christ, Father of glory, you gave your servants Joshua and Solomon the Spirit of Wisdom to enable them to lead your chosen people. I call on you now, and I ask for the gift of the Spirit of Wisdom that I may discern your will today, tomorrow, and forever. Amen.

Spirit of Understanding

Scripture: "If the great Lord is willing, he [who devotes himself to the study of the law of the Most High] will be filled with the spirit of understanding; he will pour forth words of wisdom of his own and give thanks to the Lord in prayer." (Sir 39:6)

Reflection: The author of the OT (A) book of Sirach was probably a scribe, a student of the Torah, that is, the law of the Most High, from which understanding is gleaned. After explaining the proper behavior of a scribe (Sir 38:34b—39:5), he can only rely on God's will to give him the Spirit of Understanding for which he seeks. Such a Spirit will enable him to speak words of wisdom and understanding himself, while giving thanks to God in prayer for this great gift. In the HB (OT) book of Job, Zophar the Naamathite claims to have this gift. He answers Job by saying that "a spirit beyond [his] understanding answers [him]" (Job 20:3).

It is from the prophet Isaiah that we learn about the spirit of the LORD resting on the stump of Jesse—the hoped for Davidic descendant after the Babylonian captivity—and giving him the spirit of understanding (Isa 11:2). This gift of the Holy Spirit enables us to grasp the deeper insights of faith. The meaning of living our spiritual lives through our connection with the Spirit becomes clearer and clearer to our understanding. That is why we ask God to pour a spirit of truth, understanding, and peace upon those assembled for a council or a synod and those gathered for a spiritual or pastoral meeting.[16] In the OC, God is asked to send the spirit of understanding upon those being confirmed.[17] We want to understand more deeply the meaning of spirit enabled by Spirit, because such insights will guide us deeper into the mystery of God.

---

16. "Masses and Prayers," I. For Holy Church, 5. For a Council or a Synod, Collect, 1248; 20. For a Spiritual or Pastoral Gathering, Collect, 1284.

17. OC, pars. 25, 42, 54.

Journal/Meditation: When have you experienced the Spirit of Understanding guiding you deeper into the mystery of God? Explain.

Prayer: Great Lord, you fill those who study your word with the Spirit of Understanding that they may pour forth words of insight about you and give thanks to you in prayer. Fill me with your Spirit beyond understanding that I may never to cease to praise you—Father, Son, and Holy Spirit—now and forever. Amen.

Spirit of Counsel

Scripture: "Who has directed the spirit of the LORD, or as his counselor has instructed him?" (Isa 40:13)

Reflection: In a series of questions, one of which is above, the prophet Isaiah invites his readers to consider that God, the sovereign creator of the universe, has no counselor. The prophet's words are echoed in the OT (A) book of Wisdom's question: ". . . [W]ho can learn the counsel of God? Or who can discern what the Lord wills? (Wis 9:13) In the CB (NT), Paul asks Isaiah's question this way: ". . . [W]ho has known the mind of the Lord? Or who has been his counselor?" (Rom 11:34) The Wisdom of Solomon expresses the sovereignty of God in asking, "Who has learned your counsel, unless you have given wisdom and sent your holy spirit from on high?" (Wis 9:17) This is why Isaiah says that the LORD "is wonderful in counsel, and excellent in wisdom" (Isa 28:29), and it leads the prophet to write that "the spirit of counsel" will rest upon David's successor (Isa 11:2), who will be named "Wonderful Counselor" (Isa 9:6). The psalmist echoes these words by blessing the LORD, who gives him counsel (Ps 16:7), knowing that the counsel of the LORD stands forever (Ps 33:11), and trusting that God guides him with his counsel (Ps 73:24). In Psalm 32, God says, "I will counsel you with my eye upon you" (Ps 32:8b).

The Spirit of Counsel permeates the HB (OT) book of Job. In Job, counsel is advice given in the attempt to understand Job's suffering. Job asks: "Is wisdom with the aged, and understanding in length of days?" (Job 12:12) He echoes Sirach's exclamation: "How attractive is wisdom in the aged, and understanding and counsel in the venerable!" (Sir 25:5) Job knows that God "leads counselors away stripped, and makes fools of judges" (Job 12:17). With tongue in cheek he addresses one of his friends: "How you have counseled one who has no wisdom, and given much good advice!" (Job 26:3) He reminiscences about his former life when he gave advice to others: "They listened to me, and waited, and kept silence for my counsel" (Job 29:21). When the LORD finally appears, he asks Job: "Who is this that darkens counsel by words without knowledge?" (Job 38:2) But Job asks God: "Who is this that hides counsel without knowledge?" (Job 42:3a) The author of the CB (NT) Letter to the Ephesians calms all Job's questions by stating that God accomplishes all things according to his counsel and will (Eph 1:11). The book of Proverbs is very clear about this: "No wisdom, no understanding, no counsel, can avail against the LORD" (Prov 21:30). Thus, we pray for a Spirit of Counsel;[18] we need the leadership of the Spirit for guidance in practical matters that affect our spirits in order to know the will of God.

Journal/Meditation: What counsel has your spirit received from the Spirit? Explain. How did that counsel reveal God's will to you and for you?

Prayer: No one has known your mind or given you counsel, sovereign LORD, unless you have given it by sending your Holy Spirit from on high. Send the Spirit of Counsel to rest upon me. I bless you for this gift that leads me to do your will now and forever. Amen.

Spirit of Fortitude

Scripture: "[The mother of seven dead sons] did not approve the deliverance that would preserve the seven sons for a short time, but as the daughter of God-fearing Abraham she remembered his fortitude." (4 Macc 15:28)

Reflection: In all the books—HB (OT), OT (A), and CB (NT)—in the *New Revised Standard Version* of the Bible, the word *fortitude* is found only one time in the OT (A) book of Fourth Maccabees. The mother of seven sons watches each son die rather than renege on their Jewish faith when challenged to do so by the Greek ruler Antiochus. According to Fourth Maccabees, the unnamed mother "was of the same mind as Abraham" (4 Macc 14:20), who was willing to sacrifice his son Isaac (Gen 22:1–19). Both the mother and Abraham exemplify fortitude, courage and endurance to do what God asks in the face of all obstacles, even death. Such strength and endurance in difficult or painful situations is a theme permeating Fourth Maccabees (1:11; 6:13; 7:9; 9:8, 30; 11:12,

---

18. "Proper of Saints," St. Lawrence of Brindisi, July 21, Collect, 905; "Masses and Prayers," I. For Holy Church, 3. For the Bishop, Collect, 1246; OC, pars. 25, 42, 54.

15:30; 17:2, 17, 23). Isaiah calls such endurance the spirit of might (Is 11:2).

Fortitude, in terms of endurance, makes its way into Luke's Gospel in the CB (NT) as "patient endurance" (Luke 8:15). The Lukan Jesus instructs his disciples, like the mother of seven sons, "By your endurance you will gain your souls" (Luke 21:19). In his Letter to the Romans, Paul hints at the fortitude of the mother and her seven sons when he writes about boasting in sufferings, "knowing that suffering produces endurance, and endurance produces character" (Rom 5:3–4). The author of the Letter to the Hebrews makes it very clear that one needs endurance, "so that when [one has] done the will of God, [he or she] may receive what was promised" (Heb 10:36). In a similar vein, the author of the Letter of James encourages his readers to be joyful when facing trials of any kind because "the testing of . . . faith produces endurance" (Jas 1:3). They should "let endurance have its full effect, so that [they] may be mature and complete, lacking in nothing" (Jas 1:4). However, it is the book of Revelation which comes in second place behind Fourth Maccabees for its insistence on the Spirit of Fortitude. The author calls it patient endurance, while he is exiled on Patmos because of the word of God. He expresses knowledge of the patient endurance or fortitude of others (Rev 2:2; 3:10), and he calls for the endurance and faith of the saints (Rev 13:10; 14:12). This is why we ask God to bestow the Spirit of Fortitude,[19] the courage to conquer fear, upon those about to be confirmed[20] and pray that the Spirit of Fortitude will help us know what we need to do and do it.[21] We also pray to be strengthened with the Spirit of Fortitude,[22] and we ask God to grant bishops a spirit of counsel to faithfully govern the people entrusted to their care.[23]

Journal/Meditation: When have your most recently experienced your spirit receiving the Spirit of Fortitude? What strength, might, and (patient) endurance did you have?

Prayer: God of might, you bestowed the Spirit of Fortitude upon Abraham and the mother of seven sons, giving them strength, courage, and endurance to do your will. Bestow upon me the Spirit of Fortitude

---

19. "Proper of Saints," St. Josaphat, November 12, Prayer after Communion, 994.

20. OC, pars. 25, 42, 54.

21. "Proper of Saints," St. Lawrence of Brindisi, July 21, Collect, 905.

22. Ibid., Sts. Cornelius and Cyprian, September 16, Prayer after Communion, 950.

23. "Masses and Prayers," I. For Holy Church, 3. For the Bishop, Collect, 1246.

that I may not be afraid to bear witness to the faith I profess today, tomorrow, and forever. Amen.

Spirit of Knowledge

Scripture: "God answered Solomon, 'Because this was in your heart, and you have not asked for possessions, wealth, honor, or the life of those who hate you, and have not even asked for long life, but have asked for wisdom and knowledge for yourself that you may rule my people over whom I have made you king, wisdom and knowledge are granted to you." (2 Chr 1:11–12a)

Reflection: In the Second Book of Chronicles, Solomon, David's successor to Israel's throne, prayed for wisdom and knowledge (2 Chr 1:10). And the LORD God answered his prayer by giving him the wisdom and knowledge he requested. In the OT (A) book of Wisdom, Solomon acknowledges that it is God who gave him unerring knowledge of what exists (Wis 7:17); he describes his initiation into the knowledge of God as one of the works of wisdom (Wis 8:4). Like the four young men in the HB (OT) book of Daniel, God endowed Solomon with knowledge and insight (Dan 1:4). Daniel declares that God gives "wisdom to the wise and knowledge to those who have understanding" (Dan 2:21b). The Spirit of Knowledge that Solomon describes is not information that can be garnered from school, books, teachers, computers, or smart phones. This gift of the Spirit enables us to see God reflected in all creatures and to praise him mirrored in them, while desiring God alone. The Spirit of Knowledge may be best understood as insight, the ability to see clearly and intuitively into the nature of a complex person, situation, or subject, in a way similar to way God does. There is knowledge in the Most High (Ps 73:11), who gives wisdom and knowledge and joy (Eccl 2:26). ". . . [W]ithout knowledge there is no wisdom," states Sirach (3:25). The Lord directs knowledge (Sir 39:7), but the utterance of knowledge comes from the Spirit (1 Cor 12:8). This leads Paul to exclaim: "O the depth and the riches and wisdom and knowledge of God! How unsearchable are his judgments and how inscrutable his ways!" (Rom 11:33). This leads Balaam to declare "the oracle of one who hears the words of God, and knows the knowledge of the Most High" (Num 24:16a).

The prophet Isaiah states that the Spirit of Knowledge will be given to the Davidic descendant who rules Judah after the Babylonian captivity

(Isa 11:2). The Spirit of Knowledge is the enlightenment only God has. Isaiah asks his readers about this in a question: "Who taught [the Lord GOD] knowledge, and showed him the way of understanding?" (Isa 40:14b) The answer is, of course, no one. This is why Moses tells the Israelites, "To you [terrifying displays of power were] shown so that you would acknowledge that the LORD is God" (Deut 4:35, 39). Later, Moses adds, "... [I]t is you who must acknowledge his greatness, his mighty hand and his outstretched arm" (Deut 11:2). To acknowledge God's mighty deeds is to say, "the LORD is a God of knowledge" (1 Sam 2:3). Thus, the author of the Letter to the Colossians prays that his readers "may be filled with the knowledge of God's will in all spiritual wisdom and understanding" and continue to "grow in the knowledge of God" (Col 1:9–10; 2:2). We pray that the Spirit will open to all peoples the knowledge of God,[24] that God will send the Spirit of Knowledge upon those being confirmed,[25] and that the Spirit of Knowledge will assist bishops in faithfully governing the peoples entrusted to their care.[26] The goal is to know in our spirits the God who alone gives the Spirit of Knowledge.

Journal/Meditation: When have your most recently experienced your spirit receiving the Spirit of Knowledge? What knowledge of God's will was revealed to you?

Prayer: LORD, you give wisdom to the wise and knowledge to those who have understanding. Fill me with the Spirit of Knowledge that I may know your will in all spiritual wisdom and understanding and continue to grow in love of you, who are one God—Father, Son, and Holy Spirit—forever and ever. Amen.

Spirit of Piety

Scripture: Eleazar said to the people: "[Our divine law philosophy] instructs us in justice, so that in all our dealings we act impartially, and it teaches us piety, so that with proper reverence we worship the only living God." (4 Macc 5:24).

Reflection: During the time of Greek occupation of and rule in the promised land, there was an old man named Eleazar, who was a leader of the Jews with a "reputation for piety" (4 Macc 5:18). Antiochus—the

---

24. "Pentecost Sunday," At the Mass during the Day, Preface, 454–456.
25. OC, pars. 25, 42, 54.
26. "Masses and Prayers," I. For Holy Church, 3. For the Bishop, Collect, 1246.

Greek ruler, who attempted to incorporate all Jews into Hellenism—urged Eleazar to eat meat which was forbidden by Torah. As an example to young Jews, Eleazar refuses to break Torah (4 Macc 5:25). He states, "I am not so old and cowardly as not to be young in reason on behalf of piety" (4 Macc 5:31). So, he is prepared for torture by being stripped, "though he remained adorned with the gracefulness of his piety" (4 Macc 6:2). After being killed, this aged man is praised because his piety enabled him to endure his tortures even to death (4 Macc 7:16). In the same OT (A) book, a mother with seven sons—all of whom are put to death—is praised this way: "The moon in heaven, with the stars, does not stand so august as you, who, after lighting the way of your star-like seven sons to piety, stand in honor before God and are firmly set in heaven with them" (4 Macc 17:5). At the end of Fourth Maccabees, all "Israelite children, offspring of the seed of Abraham," are told to "exercise piety in every way" (4 Macc 18:1).

From the narrative about Eleazar, we garner an understanding of the Spirit of Piety. It is a reverence for God, displayed in love. The Spirit of Piety instills zeal in prayer and worship in our spirits. It engenders observance of religious principles in our everyday lives. The Spirit of Piety is not manifest by bowed heads and folded hands without inner animation of our spirits. In the CB (NT), the Matthean Jesus emphasizes the harmony between intent and action. To those who act but have no inner motivation, he says, "Beware of practicing your piety before others in order to be seen by them; for then you have no reward from your Father in heaven" (Matt 6:1). We pray that the Spirit of Piety be given to bishops as a gift to help them govern the flock entrusted to their care.[27] We also ask God to bestow the Spirit of Piety on those being confirmed.[28] The Spirit of Piety connected to our spirits enables and leads us to reverence God authentically. Our love for the divine spills over into zeal in prayer and worship, and every day we observe the religious principles that give meaning to our lives.

Journal/Meditation: When have your most recently experienced your spirit receiving the Spirit of Piety? In what specific ways was that piety manifest?

Prayer: Almighty God, you so filled your servant Eleazar with the Spirit of Piety that he showed proper reverence to you, the only living

---

27. Ibid.
28. OC, pars. 25, 42, 54.

God, through torture to his death. As he maintained his reputation for piety, adorned with the gracefulness of the Spirit of Piety, maintain my authenticity and grant me the grace of eternal life with you and your Son, Jesus Christ, and the Holy Spirit forever and ever. Amen.

Spirit of Fear of the Lord

Scripture: "The fear of the Lord is glory and exultation, and gladness and a crown of rejoicing. The fear of the Lord delights the heart, and gives gladness and joy and long life. Those who fear the Lord will have a happy end; on the day of their death they will be blessed." (Sir 1:11–13)

Reflection: Of all the twenty-four biblical verses containing the phrase *fear of the Lord*, all but three of them are found in the OT (A) book of Sirach; there are other references, such as "The spirit of those who fear the Lord will live" (Sir 34:14), but there are twenty-one specific occurrences of the phrase *fear of the Lord* in Sirach, three of which are found in the quotation above. The basic theme concerning the fear of the Lord is that it is the beginning of wisdom (Sir 1:14; Prov 9:10), the root of wisdom (Sir 1:20), the crown of wisdom (Sir 1:18), and wisdom itself (Sir 1:27; Job 28:28); it is the beginning of acceptance, and wisdom obtains the Lord's love (Sir 19:18). According to Sirach, "The whole of wisdom is fear of the Lord . . ." (Sir 19:20), and "the fulfillment of the fear of the Lord is wisdom" (Sir 21:11b). The fear of the Lord is not to be disobeyed (Sir 1:28), but persevered in (Sir 2:10). Those who receive the Spirit of the Fear of the Lord glory in it (Sir 9:16); they are worthy of honor in God's eyes (Sir 10:20, 22). "The fear of the Lord is like a garden of blessing, and covers a person better than any glory" (Sir 40:27). Walsh says that the fear of the Lord is "a kind of gasping wonder."[29]

Even children should possess the Spirit of the Fear of the Lord (Sir 16:2), while the boast of the aged is the fear of the Lord (Sir 25:6); those who are not steadfast in the fear of the Lord have their houses quickly overthrown (Sir 27:3). The fear of the Lord is better than riches and strength (Sir 40:26a). In other words, ". . . [N]othing is better than the fear of the Lord" (Sir 23:27b), because "[t]here is no want in the fear of the Lord, and with it there is no need to seek for help" (Sir 40:26b). The "Fear of the Lord surpasses everything . . ." (Sir 25:11), so we should be zealous in it (Sir 45:33). In the HB (OT) book of Proverbs, "[t]he fear of

---

29. Walsh, *Chasing Mystery*, 63.

the LORD is the beginning of knowledge" (Prov 1:7; 2:5–6). The Spirit of the Fear of the Lord, named by the prophet Isaiah (11:2), which is the delight of the Davidic successor (Isa 11:3), becomes the way of the life of the first followers of Jesus, as is recorded in the Acts of the Apostles: "Living in the fear of the Lord and in the comfort of the Holy Spirit, [the church] increased in numbers" (Acts 9:31b). According to Paul, knowing the Spirit of the Fear of the Lord enables him to persuade others about the death and resurrection of Christ Jesus (2 Cor 5:11). Thus, we ask God to fill those being confirmed with the Spirit of the Fear of the Lord and to lead them throughout their lives with great awe and reverence.[30]

Journal/Meditation: When have your most recently experienced your spirit receiving the Spirit of the Fear of the Lord? Which biblical phrase best describes it?

Prayer: Fear of you, Lord, is the beginning of wisdom, the root of wisdom, the crown of wisdom, and wisdom itself. Fill me with the Spirit of the Fear of the Lord that I may live my life with great awe and reverence in your presence today, tomorrow, and forever. Amen.

---

30. OC, pars. 25, 42, 54.

8

Miscellaneous Spirit

Worship in Spirit

Scripture: ". . . [I]t is we who are the circumcision, who worship in the Spirit of God and boast in Christ Jesus and have no confidence in the flesh." (Phil 3:3)

Reflection: When Paul writes to the Philippians and tells them that they are the circumcision, he is not referring literally to the removal of the foreskin of the male penis, but metaphorically to them being God's people, who worship in God's Spirit. Worship here is not limited to the usual understanding of going to church or praying. It carries the wider context of serving and ministering in devotion to God, like that in which Jesus engaged. That is why Paul says to boast in Christ Jesus—who was raised from the dead to new life by the Spirit. Flesh without the animation of the Spirit offers no hope.

Worship in the Spirit, who is adored and glorified with the Father and the Son,[1] involves petitioning God for the Spirit of devotion so that people can celebrate a sacrifice pleasing to him.[2] To worship in the Spirit requires that God send the Spirit to connect to worshipers' spirits. Only God knows what worship he favors. We pray that as we approach the altar

---

1. "Order of Mass," par. 18.
2. "Common of Holy Men and Women," I. For All Categories of Saints, A. For Several Saints, 3, Prayer over the Offerings, 1100.

that God grant us the Spirit of devotion in order that we offer a worthy sacrifice.[3] We also ask that God give a newly-blessed abbess the Spirit of devoted care to the nuns entrusted to her governance.[4] Worship in Spirit flows outward in service from the individual spirit connected to the divine Spirit. When many individuals, whose spirits are connected to Spirit, gather together for worship, they form an assembly devoted to service in the broadest sense of the word. They are animated by the Spirit, who communicates to them what God desires.

Journal/Meditation: When have you most recently worshiped alone in Spirit? When have you most recently worshiped with others in Spirit? What service was the result of your devotion?

Prayer: I worship you in Spirit, O God, and I boast of you in Christ Jesus. Send your Spirit of devotion to me that I may approach you with what pleases you in service. Hear my prayer, O Holy Trinity—Father, Son, and Holy Spirit—now and forever. Amen.

Spirit of Love

Scripture: ". . . God did not give us a spirit of cowardice, but rather a spirit of power and of love and of self-discipline." (2 Tim 1:7)

Reflection: In the Second Letter to Timothy, the author reminds his readers that God gave them the Spirit of love, among other spiritual gifts. The Spirit of love is one quality—among several others—that describes a Christian. It is a gift given by God to those who believe that Jesus died and God raised him from the dead. Thus, it is present in a believer through the indwelling Spirit, and it manifests itself in good works. The author of the Letter to the Colossians states that they have this love in the Spirit (Col 1:8) and bear fruit in every good work (Col 1:10). This leads Paul in his Letter to the Romans to write: "I appeal to you, brothers and sisters, by our Lord Jesus Christ and by the love of the Spirit, to join me in earnest prayer to God on my behalf" (Rom 15:30). If all believers are united in the Spirit of love, their prayer will be heard, and Paul will be rescued from unbelievers and make his way to Rome (Rom 15:31-32).

---

3. Ibid., II. For Monks and Religious, A. For an Abbot, Prayer over the Offerings, 1104.

4. "Ritual Masses," VI. For the Blessing of an Abbot or an Abbess, 2, For the Blessing of an Abbess, Solemn Blessing, 1202.

In the RM, we ask God to raise us to new life through the love of the Spirit[5] and to pour upon us a Spirit of love for God himself.[6] We acknowledge that God fills with a Spirit of love those who pasture his people.[7] We ask God to strengthen in those who mark twenty-five or fifty years of religious profession a Spirit of perfect charity, which is another way of petitioning God for the Spirit of love.[8] Finally, we ask God to set our hearts aflame with the Spirit of charity that our thoughts will be worthy and pleasing and that our love for others will be sincere.[9] When the Spirit of Love connects to our spirits, we overflow with good works, the first of which is a deeper love for God, which itself leads to all other good works, including ministry and charity of all kinds. In giving us the Spirit of Love, God gives himself; he shares with us the very inner life of perfect charity among the persons of the Trinity.

Journal/Meditation: When have you most recently experienced the Spirit of Love inspiring your spirit to a good work of charity? How was your love for God deepened?

Prayer: Eternal God, you have not given your people a spirit of cowardice, but rather a Spirit of love. I appeal to you by my Lord Jesus Christ to pour on me the love of the Spirit that I may overflow in charity with good works. I ask this, Father, through your Son in the unity of the Holy Spirit forever and ever. Amen.

Joy in Spirit

Scripture: ". . . [T]he kingdom of God is not food and drink but righteousness and peace and joy in the Holy Spirit." (Rom 14:17)

Reflection: According to Paul in his Letter to the Romans, God's reign has nothing to do with food and drink. God is interested in people who accept his gifts of reconciliation, peace, and joy in the Spirit. This same idea is echoed by the author of Luke's Gospel. The narrator states, "At that same hour Jesus rejoiced in the Holy Spirit and said, 'I thank you,

---

5. "Proper of Time," Easter Time, Friday of the Third Week of Easter, Collect, 409.

6. "Proper of Saints," St. Camillus de Lellis, July 18, Collect, 904; "Ritual Masses," II. For the Conferral of the Sacraments of Christian Initiation,4. For the Conferral of Confirmation, C, Prayer after Communion, 1134; OC, par. 60.

7. "Common of Pastors," III. For Pastors, A. For Several Pastors, Collect, 1077.

8. "Masses and Prayers," I. For Holy Church, 13. For Religious, B, Collect, 1264.

9. Ibid., III. For Various Occasions, 40. For Charity, Collect, 1309.

Father, Lord of heaven and earth, because you have hidden these things from the wise and the intelligent and have revealed them to infants; yes, Father, for such was your gracious will'" (Luke 10:21). The feelings of great happiness or pleasure—which are hidden from the wise and intelligent but are available to children—come because Spirit is connected to spirit; this is why some things are hidden. It is the "joy inspired by the Holy Spirit" that results when we receive the word of God (1 Thess 1:6).

Paul exhorts his readers, "Do not lag in zeal, be ardent in spirit, serve the Lord" (Rom 12:11). However, joyful enthusiasm in Spirit must be authentic, as must service to the Lord. Such is not the case with the Greek ruler Antiochus, who "was elated in spirit," but "did not perceive that the Lord was angered for a little while" when he took the holy vessels from the Temple in Jerusalem (2 Macc 5:17). In other words, in his inauthentic joy of exercising his power as ruler, he did not realize that he was God's instrument for punishing the sins of his people. The OC identifies God's kingdom with joy in the Spirit.[10] Even after a person is endowed and enlightened with the gifts of the Spirit,[11] one can pray to continue to advance toward God's kingdom with a joyful spirit in the way of love.[12]

Journal/Meditation: What joy do you experience as a result of Spirit connected to spirit? How do you characterize that joy?

Prayer: Your kingdom, O God, is joy in the Spirit. Do not let me lag in zeal, but keep me ardent in spirit that I may serve you in the name of your Son, Jesus Christ, my Lord, who with you and the Holy Spirit are one God forever and ever. Amen.

Spirit of Justice

Scripture: "In that day the LORD of hosts will be . . . a spirit of justice to the one who sits in judgment . . . ." (Isa 28:5–6)

Reflection: According to the HB (OT) prophet Isaiah, the LORD of hosts—literally the Mighty God (Isa 9:5)—will fill the Judean king, who sits in judgment, with the Spirit of Justice. This Spirit defends and protects people's rights. Also, "a spirit of judgment" is the means by which the LORD cleanses Jerusalem (Isa 4:4). In his First Letter to the Corinthians,

---

10. OC, pars. 30, 47.
11. Ibid., pars. 59, 60.
12. "Common of Holy Men and Women," II. For Monks and Religious, D. For Religious, 2, Collect, 1109.

Paul employs this idea, writing, "... [Y]ou were washed, you were sanctified, you were justified in the name of the Lord Jesus Christ and in the Spirit of our God" (1 Cor 6:11b). The Corinthians, who were washed in the waters of baptism, have become God's people and have been made holy by God, who has established a relationship between them and himself. This justification came through the death and resurrection of Christ Jesus, and it continues in his spiritually, dynamic, active presence in the Spirit.

The biblical understanding of justice as giving to others what is their due in the same way that God gives to us what is our due is not the cultural definition of justice. In our culture, justice is often pictured as the blindfolded lady holding the scales. However, for most people, the scales are tipped in their direction because they want revenge. To see this truth incarnate just tune in to the national, evening news. The family of an individual, who was shot for firing on law enforcement, wants revenge in terms of prison time for the officer. A victim of a car accident wants revenge in terms of a huge sum of money because he or she presumes that he or she is due it. Parents of bullied children want revenge on the school their child attends, the principal, or the student bully. Biblical justice seeks judgment that gives everyone what is due to him or her. The goal of biblical justice is balance, not revenge, but it is not easy, either. The HB (OT) book of Proverbs puts it this way: "... [O]ne who is cool in spirit has understanding" (Prov 17:27b). Deep understanding is the work of the Spirit of Justice. The model is God, who always gives to people what is due them and never seeks to avenge himself on them. The Spirit of Justice is another way to speak about God's mercy, which, according to his justice and judgment, forgives over and over again.

Journal/Meditation: When have you most recently experienced the Spirit of Justice connected to your spirit? What was the difference between the Spirit of Justice and revenge?

Prayer: Mighty God, LORD of hosts, you are a Spirit of Justice to those who sit in judgment. Continue to wash, to sanctify, and to justify the people of the earth in the name of your Son, my Lord Jesus Christ, who lives and reigns in the Holy Spirit with you, one God, forever and ever. Amen.

Humble in Spirit

Scripture: "For thus says the high and lofty one who inhabits eternity, whose name is Holy: I dwell in the high and holy place, and also with those who are contrite and humble in spirit, to revive the spirit of the humble, and to revive the heart of the contrite." (Isa 57:15)

Reflection: According to the above verse from the HB (OT) prophet Isaiah, the Holy One, who lives on the top level of a three-storied universe, also lives on the earth, the middle level, with people who are humble—that is, of the earth—in Spirit in order to revive them. Later, God adds, ". . . [T]his is the one to whom I will look, to the humble and contrite in spirit, who trembles at my word" (Isa 66:2b). In the Prayer of Azariah, we find the young men in the furnace singing to God: ". . . [W]ith a contrite heart and a humble spirit may we be accepted" (Sg Three 1:16 [Dan 3:39]). To be humble in Spirit is to surrender to God. Surrendering to God means to let go of making a project out of life. Surrendering to God means to invite his Spirit to connect to our contrite spirits, which he revives.

Proverbs says, "It is better to be of a lowly spirit among the poor than to divide the spoil with the proud" (Prov 16:19). And in another verse Proverbs says, "A person's pride will bring humiliation, but one who is lowly in spirit will obtain honor" (Prov 28:23). A lowly spirit is being humble in Spirit. Echoing Isaiah above, it is with a humble Spirit and a contrite heart that we ask God to accept us and our gifts in the RM.[13] We also acknowledge that following Christ in poverty of Spirit and serving others in a spirit of poverty and in humility of heart is another way to be humble in Spirit.[14] And we humbly implore God in the Holy Spirit to keep us in his love.[15] Contrary to the cultural assumption that humility is letting others walk over you, being humble in Spirit is a religious claim to neutrality in the competition of life. As Proverbs makes clear, humility has precedence over honor. Humility leaves us powerless so that God's Spirit can revive our spirits.

---

13. "Order of Mass," par. 26.

14. "Proper of Saints," St. Clare, August 11, Collect, 923; "Masses and Prayers," I. For Holy Church, 13. For Religious, A, Collect, 1263.

15. "Proper of Saints," Sts. Simon and Jude, October 28, Prayer after Communion, 977.

Journal/Meditation: When have you experienced yourself possessing a humble spirit that was revived by Spirit? What cultural assumptions do you have about being humble in Spirit?

Prayer: High and lofty One who inhabits eternity, whose name is Holy, you delight in and accept those with a contrite heart and a humble spirit. I humbly implore you in the Holy Spirit to keep me in your love. Grant this through Jesus Christ, your Son, who with you and the Holy Spirit are one God forever and ever. Amen.

Broken Spirit

Scripture: "The sacrifice acceptable to God is a broken spirit; a broken and contrite heart, O God, you will not despise." (Ps 51:17)

Reflection: A broken spirit—or contrite heart—is one that is overwhelmed with sorrow of some kind. A broken spirit is a sacrifice acceptable to God, according to the psalmist, because it places spirit at the disposal of Spirit. The first response that a broken spirit gives is defense. The narrator of the HB (OT) book of Exodus states that the Hebrew slaves were not able at first to listen to Moses because of their broken spirit and cruel slavery (Exod 6:9). In the book of Deuteronomy, Moses tells the Israelites that if they do not keep the covenant, the LORD will give them a languishing spirit (Deut 28:65). Job states that as a result of his suffering, his spirit is broken (Job 17:1). Likewise, the narrator of the OT (A) Second Book of Maccabees states that the Greek ruler Antiochus was broken in spirit because of his suffering (2 Macc 9:11). The HB (OT) book of Proverbs contains many references to a broken spirit: ". . . [B]y sorrow of heart the spirit is broken" (Prov 15:13); ". . . [A] downcast spirit dries up the bones" (Prov 17:22); "The human spirit will endure sickness; but a broken spirit—who can bear?" (Prov 18:14) Even a perverseness with a gentle tongue breaks the spirit (Prov 15:4). The HB (OT) book of Daniel refers to a broken spirit as a troubled spirit (Dan 2:1, 3), and the OT (A) book of Baruch calls it a wearied spirit (Bar 3:1). In the CB (NT), the Matthean Jesus identifies the poor in spirit as blessed (Matt 5:3).

If the human spirit can be broken or in anguish, and it is animated by the Spirit, then the Spirit can be broken, wearied, or languishing, too. The Spirit longs to be connected to spirit because it gives life to spirit. When the human spirit is broken, wearied, or languishing, instead of defense it needs to submit itself to enlivening Spirit. That is why a broken spirit is the acceptable sacrifice to God. We bring our brokenness, sorrow, distress, anger, impatience—all our experiences of being battered by events in our lives—and offer them to the Spirit. Just as ancient sacrifices were transformed by fire into smoke which rose up to God, so our broken spirits are transformed into Spirit when they are offered to the LORD. God delights in inspiring broken spirits with Spirit.

Journal/Meditation: When did you last experience a broken spirit? How was it healed by the Spirit?

Prayer: O God, the sacrifice acceptable to you is a broken spirit; a broken and contrite heart, O God, you do not despise. Accept my broken spirit, and send your Spirit as a healing remedy for my spirit in the name of Jesus Christ now and forever. Amen.

Grieved in Spirit

Scripture: "On that day [when Tobit was in so much grief and anguish of heart that he prayed for death, Sarah] was grieved in spirit and wept. When she had gone up to her father's upper room, she intended to hang herself." (Tob 3:10ab)

Reflection: When a person experiences grief, he or she is in a state of great sadness. Such is the dual case of Tobit and Sarah in the OT (A) book of Tobit. Tobit is in great sadness because he is blind; he prays: O Lord, "... command my spirit to be taken from me, so that I may be released from the face of the earth and become dust" (Tob 3:6). Sarah is grieved in spirit because she has married seven husbands, and every one of them has died before their wedding night! She prays that the Lord will take her life (Tob 3:15e). Isaiah's words capture Sarah's predicament: She is "a wife forsaken and grieved in spirit" (Isa 54:6a). Isaiah also describes God's chosen people in rebellion; they "grieved his holy spirit" (Isa 63:10a). In the CB (NT), the author of the Letter to the Ephesians tells his readers, "... [D]o not grieve the Holy Spirit of God, with which you were marked with a seal for the day of redemption" (Eph 4:30). In other words, do not sadden the Spirit, who dwells within you and is connected to your spirit.

Another way of writing about being grieved in spirit is having an anguished spirit. Job speaks "in the anguish of [his] spirit" (Job 7:11), while Isaiah mentions wailing "for anguish of spirit" (Isa 65:14). The OT (A) book of Wisdom portrays the unrighteous speaking to one another in repentance "in anguish of spirit" (Wis 5:3). Feeling anguish is being tormented with grief, regret, or hopelessness. Even the Markan Jesus sighs deeply in his grieved spirit when asked for a sign from the Pharisees (Mark 8:12). The great sadness, the grief, and the anguish experienced by Tobit and Sarah is removed. Tobit's blindness is healed, and Sarah marries Tobias, Tobit's son, without him dying on their marriage night! When the grieved in spirit submit themselves to the Spirit's healing power, their sadness is removed.

Journal/Meditation: When were you most recently grieved in spirit? How did the Spirit remove your great sadness?

Prayer: Almighty God, when your people experience grief in spirit, you send the healing power of the Holy Spirit to remove their great sadness and revive them. When I am anguished in spirit, show me your mercy by sending the Spirit to me. May your holy name be blessed now and forever. Amen.

Disciplined Spirit

Scripture: "... [A] holy and disciplined spirit will flee from deceit, and will leave foolish thoughts behind, and will be ashamed of the approach of unrighteousness." (Wis 1:5)

Reflection: The internal, spiritual realm that exists within each person—what we have been referring to as spirit—is the topic of the opening verses of chapter 1 of the OT (A) book of Wisdom. The person who possesses a disciplined or controlled spirit does not mislead or trick anyone. A self-disciplined spirit does not display lack of good sense, judgment, or ridiculousness. A holy, disciplined spirit is embarrassed by sin, wickedness, or evil. This is why the author of the Second Letter to Timothy tells his readers that "God did not give us a spirit of cowardice, but rather a spirit of power and of love and of self-discipline" (2 Tim 1:7).

A self-disciplined spirit enables Paul to announce the gospel (Rom 1:9) and to declare that the glory of the Torah has been set aside in favor of "the ministry of the Spirit come in glory" (2 Cor 3:8). The author of the Acts of the Apostles narrates that the early church lived in the comfort of the Holy Spirit due to the disciplined spirits of the apostles along with Barnabas and Saul (Paul) (Acts 9:31b). We pray for a disciplined spirit—a right spirit—for those who offer gifts to God in thanksgiving for their faith.[16] A disciplined spirit is trained by Spirit to turn away from deceit,

---

16. "Votive Masses," 9. The Holy Spirit, B, Prayer over the Offerings, 1341.

to flee foolish ideas, and to be embarrassed by anything that is not in harmony with Holy Spirit.

Journal/Meditation: On a scale of one to ten, how disciplined is your spirit? What do you need to do to respond better to the Spirit in terms of deceit, foolish thoughts, and sin?

Prayer: O God, you give your people the Spirit of self-discipline that they may announce the gospel of your Son's death and resurrection. Train my spirit with your Spirit that I may always possess a disciplined spirit. I ask this through my Lord Jesus Christ, who lives and reigns with you and the Holy Spirit, one God, forever and ever. Amen.

9

Evil Spirit

Blasphemy against the Spirit

Scripture: ". . . [W]hoever blasphemes against the Holy Spirit can never have forgiveness, but is guilty of an eternal sin." (Mark 3:29)

Reflection: In Mark's Gospel, the scribes declare that Jesus has Beelzebul, the ruler of demons, and by Beelzebul he casts out demons (Mark 3:22). In other words, the scribes think that Jesus is possessed or infested with Beelzebul. However, he explains the impossibility of Satan, who has become identified with Beelzebul, casting out himself (Mark 3:23). At this point in Mark's Gospel, Jesus has been casting out unclean or demonic spirits of all kinds. The blasphemy against the Holy Spirit is attributing the liberating and healing activity of Jesus to demonic power instead of recognizing that he does so because he possesses the Spirit (Mark 1:10). Such blasphemy is unforgivable because the scribes, who charge Jesus with demonic possession, see goodness as evil and are closed to the action of God's Spirit, which is manifesting itself through Jesus' activity of casting out unclean or demonic spirits.

The author of Matthew's Gospel reports that Jesus was called Beelzebul (Matt 10:25). His opponents, the Pharisees, declare that it is by the ruler of the demons that he casts out the demons (Matt 12:24). The Matthean Jesus makes explicit what the Markan Jesus leaves vague: ". . . [I]f it is by the Spirit of God that I cast out demons, then the kingdom of

God has come to you" (Matt 12:28). Then, as Matthew's Markan source states, Jesus says: ". . . I tell you, people will be forgiven for every sin and blasphemy, but blasphemy against the Holy Spirit will not be forgiven" (Matt 12:31). The Matthean Jesus adds: ". . . [W]hoever speaks [a word] against the Holy Spirit will not be forgiven either in this age or in the age to come" (Matt 12:32). In Luke's version of this account, members of a crowd witnessing Jesus cast out a demon declare that he casts it out by Beelzebul (Luke 14:15). The Lukan Jesus declares, ". . . [I]f it is by the finger of God that I cast out the demons, then the kingdom of God has come to you" (Luke 11:20). Later, the Lukan Jesus states, ". . . [W]hoever blaspheme against the Holy Spirit will not be forgiven" (Luke 12:10). It is through the Spirit that Jesus heals spirits. Demonic spirits are driven away by the Spirit-wielding Jesus. The kingdom of God is made present when Spirit heals spirit.

Journal/Meditation: Most recently when has your spirit been healed by the Spirit? What kind of healing was it?

Prayer: It was by your finger, O God, that your Son, Jesus, cast out demons, brought healing to human spirit, and announced the presence of your kingdom. Protect me from blasphemy against your Holy Spirit and keep me from uttering a word against the Holy Spirit that I may glory in your eternal presence in the age to come forever. Amen.

Evil Spirit

Scripture: ". . . God sent an evil spirit between Abimelech and the lords of Shechem; and the lords of Shechem dealt treacherously with Abimelech." (Judg 9:23)

Reflection: Abimelech is the son of Gideon (otherwise known as Jerubbaal) in the HB (OT) book of Judges. After he kills his seventy brothers, Abimelech is made king by the lords of Shechem and rules for three years. But his evil deed is punished by God, who sends an evil spirit to create an atmosphere of mutual distrust between Abimelech and the lords of Shechem. More killing results, until Abimelech himself is killed by a woman with a millstone and the sword of his armor bearer. "Thus God repaid Abimelech for the crime he committed against his father in killing his seventy brothers" (Judg 9:56). While it may seem like nonsense to modern readers, the idea that God sends an evil spirit is a firm biblical idea. If God is in charge of everything, then he is also in charge of an evil spirit. In biblical thought, God is all-powerful, and an evil spirit is another of his creation designed to do his will. This is presented most eloquently in the Second Book of Kings in which God speaks through the prophet Isaiah to King Hezekiah of Judah when he is under Assyrian siege: "Thus says the LORD: Do not be afraid because of the words that you have heard, with which the servants of the king of Assyria have reviled me. I myself will put a spirit in him, so that he shall hear a rumor and return to his own land; I will cause him to fall by the sword in his own land" (2 Kgs 19:6–7).

We find the HB (OT) book of First Samuel filled with God sending evil spirits. "Now the spirit of the LORD departed from Saul [, king of Israel], and an evil spirit from the LORD tormented him," states the narrator of First Samuel" (1 Sam 16:14). In the stories that follow, the evil spirit from God is mentioned five more times (1 Sam 16:15, 16, 23; 18:10; 19:9). In the OT (A) book of Tobit, Azariah (the angel Raphael in disguise) gives Tobias, son of Tobit, the formula to drive away an evil spirit: "As for the fish's heart and liver, you must burn them to make a smoke in the presence of a man or woman afflicted by a demon or evil spirit, and every affliction will flee away and never remain with that person any longer" (Tob 6:8). In the CB (NT), the author of Matthew's Gospel presents Jesus casting out demons by the Spirit of God as a demonstration that God's kingdom has arrived (Matt 12:28). The author of Luke's Gospel mentions that Jesus cured many people of evil spirits (Luke 7:21; 8:2), and in the second volume, the Acts of the Apostles, he describes Paul casting out evil spirits (Acts 16:18; 19:12), while itinerant Jewish exorcists are unable to do so because they know neither Jesus nor Paul (Acts 19:13–16). God's Spirit is so strong in Jesus and Paul that evil spirits cannot withstand it, even those evil spirits sent by God. In other words, Spirit drives out evil spirits.

Journal/Meditation: Have you ever encountered an evil spirit? What was its source? How did you rid yourself of it?

Prayer: All-powerful God, you send evil spirits to punish evil deeds. You sent Jesus, your Son, with your Spirit to cast our evil spirits and enact the presence of your kingdom. Grant that I may one day share in the fullness of that kingdom, where you live and reign as Father, Son, and Holy Spirit, one God, forever and ever. Amen.

Unclean Spirit

Scripture: "On that day, says the LORD of hosts, I will cut off the names of the idols from the land, so that they shall be remembered no more; and also I will remove from the land the prophets and the unclean spirit." (Zech 13:2)

Reflection: God promises to remove corruption from within Judah in the HB (OT) prophet Zechariah. In particular he declares that he will remove the prophets who possess unclean spirits, that is, those who have unclean breath, the source of the prophets' false inspiration. In the CB (NT), Mark's Gospel is full of unclean spirits, a common designation for a demon. For the author of the oldest gospel, an unclean spirit is one that is opposed to the holy; it is out of place; it is something that should not be. The Markan Jesus rebukes an unclean spirit in a man, and it comes out of him (Mark 1:23, 26). Mark records that some people thought Jesus had an unclean spirit (Mark 3:30), even though the unclean spirits fell down before Jesus when they saw him (Mark 3:11). Jesus commands the unclean spirit of a man who lives in the Gerasene tombs to come out of him (Mark 5:2, 8), and he sends it into a herd of swine (Mark 5:12–13). A Gentile woman with a little daughter, who has an unclean spirit, is granted her request when Jesus frees her daughter from the demon (Mark 7:25–30). Likewise, a man, who has a son with an unclean spirit, is cured of his unclean spirit by Jesus (Mark 9:17–29), who had given his disciples authority over unclean spirits (Mark 6:7), but they were not able to get rid of this one.

The author of Matthew's Gospel maintains that Jesus gave his twelve disciples authority over unclean spirits (Matt 10:1), but he does not narrate Jesus casting out any! He does, however, include Jesus' reflection on what happens to unclean spirits: "When the unclean spirit has gone out of a person, it wanders through waterless regions looking for a resting place, but it finds none. Then it says, 'I will return to my house from which I came.' When it comes, it finds it empty, swept, and put in order. Then it goes and brings along seven other spirits more evil than itself, and they enter and live there; and the last state of that person is worse than the first" (Matt 12:43–45a). The author of Luke's Gospel rewrites the narrative about an unclean spirit in a man, naming it the spirit of an unclean demon (Luke 4:33), it comes out of him, (Luke 4:35), and it presents the occasion for the crowd to declare that Jesus wields authority and power over unclean spirits (Luke 4:36b). Later, the narrator states that Jesus cures all who are troubled with unclean spirits (Luke 6:18). In the narrative about the Gerasene man who had demons, Jesus commands the unclean spirit to come out of him (Luke 8:29), but the rest of the story employs the word *demon* to describe Mark's unclean spirit. Likewise, Jesus rebukes the unclean spirit in a man's son, who is often seized by a spirit (Luke 9:39, 42b). Because Luke not only shares Mark's Gospel as a source with Matthew, but also another source named Q(uelle), his gospel contains a statement about the fate of unclean spirits like Matthew's Gospel does: "When the unclean spirit has gone out of a person, it wanders through waterless regions looking for a resting place, but not finding any, it says, 'I will return to my house from which I came.' When it comes, it finds it swept and put in order. Then it goes and brings seven other spirits more evil than itself, and they enter and live there; and the last state of that person is worse than the first" (Luke 11:24–26). Thus, according to biblical literature, that which is opposed to the holy is named an unclean spirit; it is out of place; it is something that should not be.

Journal/Meditation: Have you ever encountered an unclean spirit? To what holiness was it opposed? Once you rid yourself of it, did it ever return?

Prayer: Lord Jesus, you taught your disciples that unclean spirits are driven out by prayer, and, through your ministry, you enacted this truth. Remove from me any unclean spirit of whose presence I am not aware, and fill me with the Spirit of holiness that you share with your Father now and forever. Amen.

Seized by a Spirit

Scripture: "Someone from the crowd answered [Jesus], 'Teacher, I brought you my son; he has a spirit that makes him unable to speak; and whenever it seizes him, it dashes him down; and he foams and grinds his teeth and becomes rigid . . . .'" (Mark 9:17–18)

Reflection: Immediately after the account of the transfiguration, the author of Mark's Gospel presents a story about a man with an epileptic son whom Jesus' disciples are unable to heal because of their inability to pray (Mark 9:29)! "When the spirit saw [the boy], immediately it convulsed the boy, and he fell on the ground and rolled about, foaming at the mouth" (Mark 9:20b). Jesus commands the spirit to leave the boy and never enter him again (Mark 9:25). Again, the spirit convulses him terribly and comes out which leads many to think that he is dead. But Jesus lifts him up to show everyone that he is alive (Mark 9:26–27). The author of Luke's Gospel rewrites his Markan source. The boy's father says, "Teacher, I beg you to look at my son; he is my only child. Suddenly a spirit seizes him, and all at once he shrieks. It convulses him until he foams at the mouth; it mauls him and will scarcely leave him" (Luke 9:38–39). Quickly, Jesus heals the boy (Luke 9:41b–42). In another story, unique to Luke's Gospel, a woman appears "with a spirit that had crippled her for eighteen years" (Luke 13:11). The crippling spirit has bent her over so that she was unable to stand up, but Jesus heals her (Luke 13:12–13).

The account of people seized by a spirit that removes the ability to speak and to stand upright demonstrates how the spirit transforms a person into someone unrecognizable. This kind of evil is commonplace. Today we know it as epilepsy and osteoporosis, and both are treated with modern medicine which was not available in Jesus' time. Two thousand years ago, people thought that demonic spirits could invade humans and take over personalities. They could initiate the attack on a person and cause mental illness, physical diseases, deafness, and blindness. In Mark's Gospel and in Luke's Gospel, Jesus is portrayed as a divine physician who exorcises seizing spirits in enacting the kingdom of God. One possible origin of saying "God bless you" or "Bless you" after a person sneezes is that ancient people thought one was ejecting a spirit attempting to seize a person. While Pope Gregory I (Gregory the Great) is attributed with suggesting "God bless you" after a person sneezed in the hopes of protection from the sixth-century CE bubonic plague because sneezing is one obvious symptom of one form of the plague, his source is most likely the ancient understanding of expulsion of spirits with a sneeze.

Journal/Meditation: Have you ever been seized by a spirit that transformed you unrecognizably? Explain. How were you treated medically?

Prayer: Lord Jesus Christ, when you saw a spirit seize a boy and convulse him and when you met a woman crippled by a spirit, you healed them with the Spirit of God. Look upon my diseases and send the healing Spirit to my spirit. You are the divine physician now and forever. Amen.

Fainting Spirit

Scripture: "I think of God, and I moan; I meditate, and my spirit faints." (Ps 77:3)

Reflection: A spirit that faints is one that is not bright, clear, or loud. It can be unenthusiastic, without conviction. One with a fainting spirit can become dizzy, weak, or unconscious. The psalmist, who is in some kind of unidentified trouble, prays during the night, but receives no comfort (Ps 77:1-2). He thinks about God, but moans in his anguish. He reflects, but he receives no insight and remains unable to sleep or to speak (Ps 77:4). In other words, his spirit faints within him. In Psalm 142, faint indicates the need which God knows: "When my spirit is faint, you know my way," sings the psalmist (Ps 142:3). In other words, in his weak supplication to the LORD, God already knows what he needs. In Psalm 143, faintness of spirit—"Therefore my spirit faints within me; my heart within me is appalled" (Ps 143:4)—leads to the psalmist's recollection of God's past deeds and works on behalf of those who were oppressed. Nevertheless, he states, "Answer me quickly, O LORD; my spirit fails" (Ps 143:7).

The prophet Isaiah identifies "the mantle of praise instead of a faint spirit" (Isa 61:3b) as one of the gifts that the Lord GOD would bestow upon mourners in Jerusalem. However, the prophet Ezekiel is instructed by God to face Jerusalem and moan over her destruction: "Every heart will melt and all hands will be feeble, every spirit will faint, and all knees will turn to water" (Ezek 21:7b). Because of Jerusalem's rebellion against her Babylonian overlord, the spirit of her citizens will faint. In a similar manner, the author of the Letter of Jude writes about "worldly people, devoid of the Spirit, who [cause] divisions" (Jude 1:19). When spirits faint, they are devoid of Spirit; they need God to nourish and renew them with the sustenance that does not fail in body or in spirit.[1]

Journal/Meditation: When have you most recently experienced a fainting spirit? What caused your spirit to faint? How was your fainting spirit renewed by the Spirit?

Prayer: I think of you, O God, and I meditate on your words, but from time to time my spirit faints within me. You know my way. Do not leave me devoid of Spirit, but answer me quickly, O LORD, and then receive my praise forever. Amen.

---

1. "Masses and Prayers," II. For Civil Needs, 26. For the Sanctification of Human Labor, A, Prayer over the Offerings, 1290.

Troubled Spirit

Scripture: "In the morning [Pharaoh's] spirit was troubled; so he sent and called for all the magicians of Egypt and all its wise men. Pharaoh told them his dreams, but there was no one who could interpret them to Pharaoh." (Gen 41:8)

Reflection: The Pharaoh of Egypt has two dreams; one is about seven ugly and thin cows eating seven sleek and fat cows. The other is about seven full ears of plump and good grain being swallowed by seven ears of thin and blighted grain (Gen 41:1–7). After awakening from his dreams Pharaoh has a troubled spirit because he does not know what his dreams mean. We find Daniel in the same position as Pharaoh. The prophet has a vision of four beasts, an Ancient One, and a human being (Dan 7:1–14). "As for me, Daniel, my spirit was troubled within me, and the visions of my head terrified me" (Dan 7:15). Then, Daniel states that he needs an interpreter, an angel, to help him understand his vision (Dan 7:16). One who is troubled in spirit, like Pharaoh and Daniel, experiences worry or distress; a troubled spirit is prone to emotional conflict and can be calmed only by someone who ministers to it with Spirit, as does Joseph for Pharaoh and the attendant angel for Daniel.

In the CB (NT) we find the Johannine Jesus troubled or disturbed in spirit. When he approaches the tomb of his friend Lazarus, he sees Lazarus's sister, Mary, weeping "and the Jews who came with her also weeping, [and] he was greatly disturbed in spirit and deeply moved," according to the gospel's narrator (John 11:33). In the same gospel as Jesus approaches the hour of his death, he states, "Now my soul is troubled. And what should I say—'Father, save me from this hour'? No, it is for this reason that I have come to this hour" (John 12:27). Before eating a final meal with his followers, while knowing that one would betray him, the Johannine narrator states that Jesus was troubled in spirit again (John 13:21). The Spirit, whom John the Baptist testifies descended on and remains in Jesus (John 1:33), ministers to Jesus' spirit both when he is troubled and as he gives it up in death (John 19:30b). But three days later, the inspired Jesus, now raised from the dead, breathes the Spirit into the troubled-in-spirit disciples (John 20:22). In the words of Paul, the disciples have been cleansed of every defilement of spirit, making holiness perfect in the fear of God (2 Cor 7:1).

Journal/Meditation: What has been your most recent experience of having a troubled spirit? Who ministered Spirit to you? What new life did your troubled spirit receive from Spirit?

Prayer: Heavenly Father, you sent Joseph to Pharaoh and an angel to Daniel with your Spirit to calm their troubled spirits. Make holiness perfect in me by sending the Holy Spirit to renew me in the resurrected life of your Son, Jesus Christ, who is Lord forever and ever. Amen.

Proud Spirit

Scripture: "Better is the end of a thing than its beginning; the patient in spirit are better than the proud in spirit." (Eccl 7:8)

Reflection: The wisdom of the HB (OT) book of Ecclesiastes explains that it is much easier to end something than it is to get it started. Such truth is paired with identifying those who are patient in spirit as being better than those who are proud in spirit. The prophet Habakkuk also emphasizes this: "Look at the proud!" he writes. "Their spirit is not right in them, but the righteous live by their faith" (Hab 2:4). Those who have a healthy relationship with God are not proud; they live in faithfulness, firmness, steadfastness, and fidelity to the LORD. Those who are proud are pleased and satisfied with themselves because they consider that they have done something well. The proud may also be arrogant; they have an exaggerated opinion of their personal worth and abilities. In other words, they possess little to no humility.

Habakkuk's words become a wisdom saying in the book of Proverbs: "Pride goes before destruction and a haughty spirit before a fall" (Prov 16:18). Those who are condescending or arrogant—in other words, those who possess a proud spirit—usually engineer their own destruction or downfall. The HB (OT) book of Numbers gives such an example, identifying pride as a spirit of jealousy that comes upon a married man (Num 5:14, 30). While the narrative betrays a patriarchal society and functions as a means of divining whether or not a wife has had intercourse with a man other than her husband (Num 5:11–31), the point remains: A proud or a haughty spirit brings destruction, while a patient and humble spirit opens a person to the Spirit. A proud spirit is an evil spirit; a patient and righteous spirit lives by trust in the Spirit.

Journal/Meditation: Have you ever had a proud spirit? What destruction did it bring to you? How was a patient and righteous spirit given to you by the Spirit?

Prayer: LORD God, in your wisdom you have declared that the patient in spirit are better than the proud in spirit. Give to me a humble spirit that I may live in faithfulness, steadfastness, and fidelity to your Spirit now and forever. Amen.

Bitter Spirit

Scripture: "David was in great danger; for the people spoke of stoning him, because all the people were bitter in spirit for their sons and daughters. But David strengthened himself in the LORD his God." (1 Sam 30:6)

Reflection: The narrator of the First Book of Samuel writes about the danger that David—not yet king of Israel—faced because of an Amalekite attack on a city named Ziklag. The Amalekites had burned the city and taken captive all the women and children, including David's two wives (1 Sam 30:1–5). David is in danger because he has failed as a leader to protect adequately the women and children of the city. Thus, the people with David speak of stoning him because they are bitter in spirit for their children, who have been taken captive by their enemy. In other words, those who have not been taken captive are angry and resentful and find this situation difficult to accept. These folks are like the Israelites under Moses' care who so "angered the LORD at the waters of Meribah" that "it went ill with Moses on their account; for they made his spirit bitter, and he spoke words that were rash" (Ps 106:32–33).

In the OT (A) Wisdom of Jesus Son of Sirach (Ecclesiasticus), the reader is told: "Do not ridicule a person who is embittered in spirit, for there is One who humbles and exalts" (Sir 7:11). This practical advice is meant to deter one from mocking another who is angry, resentful, or finds something difficult to accept. Why? It only adds more fuel to the flames. And we do not know if it is God humbling the person or not. In a similar vein is advice given in a later chapter in Sirach: "Wine drunk to excess leads to bitterness of spirit, to quarrels and stumbling" (Sir 31:29). Here the focus is on drunkenness, which leads to anger, resentfulness, and difficulty in accepting certain events in one's life manifested by quarrels and stumbling around. The God who humbles with a bitter spirit also exalts with his Spirit. David defeats the Amalekites and rescues all the captives, because the LORD gave his enemies into his hand (1 Sam 30:16–24). The best remedy for a bitter spirit is breathing in a good dose of Spirit.

Journal/Meditation: When have you most recently experienced yourself having a bitter spirit? How was your bitter spirit transformed by Spirit?

Prayer: LORD, at the waters of Meribah it went ill with your servant Moses, whose spirit was made bitter on account of the grumbling of your chosen people. Give me the grace of the Spirit to meet anger with joy, resentfulness with acceptance, and difficulties in life with awareness that you are with me always: today, tomorrow, and forever. Amen.

Crushed in Spirit

Scripture: "The LORD is near to the brokenhearted, and saves the crushed in spirit." (Ps 34:18)

Reflection: The psalmist declares that God is present to those who are experiencing extreme sadness; however, an experience of great disappointment is not the usual event in which people presume the LORD to be. Likewise, God saves those who have had an experience that overwhelmed or defeated them; again, the experience of being crushed in spirit in not the usual event in which people presume the LORD to be. The First Book of Maccabees in the OT (A) gives the example of Judas Maccabeus, commander of the Jewish army around 160 BCE: "When Judas saw that his army had slipped away and the battle [with the army of Bacchides] was imminent, he was crushed in spirit, for he had no time to assemble them" (1 Macc 9:7). Without an army, Judas cannot defeat his enemy, but demonstrates his honor by fighting until many of his men and he were killed.

A different kind of crushed spirit appears in a reflection in the OT (A) book of Wisdom. The writer presents unsound reasoning that is presented by the ungodly: "... [W]e were born by mere chance, and hereafter we shall be as though we had never been, for the breath in our nostrils is smoke, and reason is a spark kindled by the beating of our hearts; when it is extinguished, the body will turn to ashes, and the spirit will dissolve like empty air" (Wis 2:2–3). Of course, such reasoning is false; we are not born by chance, but by the deliberate plan of God; the breath in our nostrils is not smoke, but Spirit, the animating source of life, that never dies even if the body does. In the CB (NT), Paul tells the Thessalonians pointedly, "Do not quench the Spirit" (1 Thess 5:19). Using the fire-like imagery for the Spirit, Paul tells the Thessalonians not to use water to put out the Spirit's fire in the community, especially the words of prophets through whom the Spirit speaks (1 Thess 5:20). This may be the way that God refreshes the crushed in spirit. Even in moments of extreme sadness, overwhelming defeat, or even death, Spirit is near to renew spirit.

Journal/Meditation: When have you experience extreme sadness, great disappointment, or overwhelming defeat? How did Spirit heal your crushed spirit?

Prayer: LORD, you are near to the brokenhearted, and you save the crushed in spirit. When I am sad, disappointed, or defeated, send your Spirit to revive my spirit to keep me connected to you, the source of all life, now and forever. Amen.

Downcast in Spirit

Scripture: "A cheerful heart is a good medicine, but a downcast spirit dries up the bones." (Prov 17:22)

Reflection: The first half of the above proverb declares joy to be good medicine. There is a healing effect when people are joyful. Joy invigorates; doctors know that it is important for a patient's recovery. It both preserves and restores health, while it also resists disease. Thus, good medicine is joy. By pondering all the good God has done, rather than taking the drugs of sadness or depression, we can enter into the joy of the LORD. But in the second half of the proverb, we are told that a downcast spirit dries up one's bones. This is attempting to say that a dejected spirit robs us of our strength, stability, and blood production—in a word, our very frame. With dried bones we die; our vitality is zapped by sorrow; and our spirits need an infusion of joy from the Spirit. We are reminded of the prophet Ezekiel's narrative about the valley full of dry bones which come to life with the Spirit of God (Ezek 37:1–14).

In the CB (NT), Paul explains why some of his own people, the Jews, have not accepted the grace offered to them. He doesn't blame them; rather, he states, "God gave them a sluggish spirit . . ." (Rom 11:8). Paul is recalling Moses' words to the Israelites: ". . . [T]he LORD has not given you a mind to understand . . ." (Deut 29:4). Likewise, when explaining how his readers are unable to discern God's purpose, the prophet Isaiah describes it as drunken staggering: "Stupefy yourself and be in a stupor .... For the LORD has poured out upon you a spirit of deep sleep ..." (Isa 29:9a, 10a). The words of the author of the Second Letter to Timothy seek to avoid downcast spirits in his community: "... God did not give us a spirit of cowardice," he writes, "but rather a spirit of power and of love and of self-discipline" (2 Tim 1:7). This is similar to saying that the joy-filled Spirit is good medicine for a downcast spirit.

Journal/Meditation: Most recently, when you have you experienced yourself having a downcast spirit? How did the good medicine of joy restore you? What was the source of your joy?

Prayer: Ever-joyful God, you have given your people the Spirit of power, love, and self-discipline as good medicine. When I am downcast in spirit, save me with your Spirit, and I will rejoice in you, Father, Son, and Holy Spirit, one God, forever and ever. Amen.

Lying Spirit

Scripture: "... Micaiah said, 'Therefore hear the word of the LORD: I saw the LORD sitting on his throne, with all the host of heaven standing beside him to the right and to the left of him. And the LORD said, "Who will entice [King] Ahab [of Israel], so that he may go up and fall at Ramoth-gilead?" Then one said one thing, and another said another, until a spirit came forward and stood before the LORD, saying, "I will entice him." "How?" the LORD asked him. He replied, "I will go out and be a lying spirit in the mouth of all his prophets." Then the LORD said, "You are to entice him, and you shall succeed; go out and do it." So you see, the LORD has put a lying spirit in the mouth of all these your prophets; the LORD has decreed disaster for you.'" (1 Kgs 22:19–23; 2 Chr 18:18–22)

Reflection: The passage above may be best understood by imagining dueling prophets. On one side are the court prophets of King Ahab of Israel; they tell him whatever they think he wants to hear. On the other side is the lone prophet Micaiah, who can speak only what the LORD says to him. Micaiah's vision presents God sitting on his throne surrounded by his advisers. God asks them to devise a plan in which Ahab will fall in a battle and be killed. The plan is simple: The court prophets will be possessed by a lying spirit to which Ahab will listen. He does, and he dies in battle (1 Kgs 29:29–40; 2 Chr 18:28–34). While it may not be heard well by modern ears, the biblical story identifies the LORD as giving permission for the lying spirit. Why? In biblical understanding, God is in charge of all, even lying spirits! The modern concept of an evil spirit as God's equal rival has not yet emerged. Even the prophet Isaiah delivers the word of the LORD to King Hezekia: "I myself will put a spirit in [the king of Assyria], so that he shall hear a rumor, and return to his own land; I will cause him to fall by the sword in his own land" (Isa 37:7).

In the CB (NT) book of the Acts of the Apostles, it is Satan who fills the hearts of the married couple of Ananias and his wife Sapphira "to lie to the Holy Spirit" (Acts 5:3). Peter confronts Ananias, stating, "You did not lie to us but to God!" (Acts 5:4d) Then, he confronts Sapphira, "How is it that you have . . . put the Spirit of the Lord to the test?" (Acts 5:9a) The author of the Letter to the Ephesians refers to this as "the spirit that is now at work among those who are disobedient" (Eph 2:2). A Collect in the RM reflects a later understanding of God, who is peace itself. A spirit of discord cannot grasp him, and a violent mind cannot receive him.[2] A lying spirit must be confronted with the Spirit of truth, as does Micaiah and Peter.

Journal/Meditation: Have you ever experienced a lying spirit in yourself or in another? Explain. Who confronted the lying spirit? What was the result?

Prayer: God of peace, you use a lying spirit to advance the steps of your plan, but in you there is no spirit of discord. When I find a lying spirit, give me the help of your Holy Spirit that I may persevere in what is good. I ask this through my Lord Jesus Christ now and forever. Amen.

Hardened Spirit

Scripture: Moses said, ". . . King Sihon [of the Amorites who reigned] in Heshbon was not willing to let us pass through, for the LORD your God had hardened his spirit and made his heart defiant in order to hand him over to you, as he has now done." (Deut 2:30)

Reflection: In his recounting of Israelite history, Moses reminds his people that even though he had asked for safe passage through the wilderness of Kedemoth, God had hardened the spirit of King Sihon and made him resistant to the terms of peace Moses offered. According to the author of the HB (OT) book of Deuteronomy, God is in full control of

---

2. "Masses and Prayers," II. For Civil Needs, 30. For the Preservation of Peace and Justice, B, Collect, 1298.

events surrounding his chosen people's journey from Mount Horeb (Sinai) to the Jordan River. He hardens a king's spirit just like he hardened a Pharaoh's heart (Exod 10:20, 27; 11:10). When speaking to Belshazzar, the prophet Daniel reminds him about one of his predecessors: ". . . [W]hen [Nebuchadnezzar's] heart was lifted up and his spirit was hardened so that he acted proudly, he was deposed from this kingly throne, and his glory was stripped from him . . . until he learned that the Most High God has sovereignty over the kingdom of mortals, and sets over it whomever he will" (Dan 5:20-21). The purpose of a hardened spirit is to lead one to the Spirit of God.

The prophet Hosea writes about the hardened spirit of Israel—in terms of idolatry—using the image of prostitution. According to the word of the LORD, ". . . [A] spirit of whoredom has led [the people] astray, and they have played the whore, forsaking their God" (Hos 4:12b). Later, the prophet adds, ". . . [T]he spirit of whoredom is within them, and they do not know the LORD" (Hos 5:4). Just like someone can be paid for sexual intercourse, Hosea declares that Israel's spirit is so hardened that the people pay worship to idols; both violate the covenant; both indicate that Israel has departed from God (Hos 9:1), but his compassion grows warm and tender and he will take back his rebellious children (Hos 11:1-11). In the HB (OT) book of Job, Eliphaz attacks Job's motives, asking, "Why does your heart carry you away, . . . so that you turn your spirit against God, and let such words go out of your mouth?" (Job 15:12-13) In the CB (NT), the author of the First Letter of John refers to a hardened spirit as "the spirit of the antichrist" (1 John 4:3b). This author cautions his readers not to believe every spirit, "but [to] test the spirits to see whether they are from God" (1 John 4:1). Then, he explains how to know if the Spirit of God is speaking: "[E]very spirit that confesses that Jesus Christ has come in the flesh is from God, and every spirit that does not confess Jesus is not from God" (1 John 4:2-3a). Thus, even though a hardened spirit may be God's way of directing world events and turning his people back to him, the final purpose is to separate those who acknowledge the incarnation of God's Son from those who do not. The softening of a hardened spirit is done by the Spirit.

Journal/Meditation: Have you ever experienced yourself or someone else having a hardened spirit? Explain. What was God doing by hardening your spirit or another's spirit?

Prayer: LORD, you hardened the spirit of Pharaoh and kings, making their hearts defiant, in order to preserve your chosen people. You hardened the spirit of Israel and Job in order to demonstrate your compassion and forgiveness. Soften my hardened spirit with your Spirit that I may always proclaim that Jesus Christ has come in the flesh and lives and reigns with you and the Holy Spirit, one God, forever and ever. Amen.

Spirit of Confusion

Scripture: "The LORD has poured into [the princes of Egypt] a spirit of confusion." (Isa 19:14a)

Reflection: According to the prophet Isaiah, God is responsible for the confusion found in Egypt. The LORD has caused the country to become lazy in terms of work. In this oracle concerning Egypt, Isaiah portrays God pitting Egyptian against Egyptian so that "the spirit of the Egyptians within them will be emptied out," and God "will confound their plans" (Isa 19:3a). Even the princes of Egypt are declared to be utterly foolish; those who are supposed to be wise counselors to Pharaoh give stupid counsel (Isa 19:11–13). In all its endeavors, no matter if they begin at the top or the bottom, the spirit of confusion will rule because Egypt has not come to the aid of Judah and her enemies (Isa 19:14–15).

In the CB (NT) book of the Acts of the Apostles, Stephen refers to the high priest and the members of his council as stiff-necked people who "are forever opposing the Holy Spirit, just as [their] ancestors used to do" (Acts 7:51). By opposing the Spirit and by opposing Stephen, who is filled with the Holy Spirit (Acts 7:55), they bring the spirit of confusion upon themselves and others. In his Letter to the Galatians, Paul specifies that "what the flesh desires is opposed to the Spirit, and what the Spirit desires is opposed to the flesh" (Gal 5:17). According to Paul, these are opposed to each other because dwelling in the realm of the Spirit is to be in Christ, whereas dwelling in the realm of the flesh is to be in unredeemed humanity. The Galatians cannot do whatever they want (Gal 5:17) because they must choose either the realm of the Spirit, where there is no spirit of confusion, or the realm of the flesh, where there is the spirit of confusion. In the Letter to the Hebrews, the author refers to choosing the spirit of confusion as outraging the Spirit of grace (Heb 10:29). God, who is in charge of all, sends the spirit of confusion upon those who oppose his Spirit. The divine Spirit opposes the confusion of spirit that lives in the realm of the flesh.

Journal/Meditation: When have you most recently experienced the spirit of confusion? Narrate the event. Was the spirit of confusion from God to teach you a truth? Explain. How did God's Spirit replace your spirit of confusion with truth?

Prayer: Almighty Father, those who oppose your people are often opposing your Spirit and bringing the spirit of confusion upon themselves and others. Keep me dwelling in the realm of the Spirit through Jesus Christ, your Son, who lives and reigns with you and the Holy Spirit, one God, forever and ever. Amen.

Testing the Spirit

Scripture: "... Peter said to [Sapphira], 'How is it that you have agreed ... to put the Spirit of the Lord to the test?'" (Acts 5:9a)

Reflection: When it comes to testing the Spirit, there is a negative side, and there is a positive side. The negative side is illustrated by the unique account of Ananias and his wife, Sapphira, who sell some real estate and pretend to give all the proceeds of the sale to the apostles. Peter accuses Ananias of lying to the Holy Spirit, and he falls down and dies (Acts 5:1–6). When Sapphira comes onto the scene three hours later, Peter asks her why she put the Spirit to the test, then, like her husband, she falls down and dies (Acts 5:7–11). The conspiracy to lie to the community, whose members freely sold their property and gave the proceeds to the apostles for the benefit of all (Acts 4:32–37), by pretending to donate all the proceeds of the sold property tests the Spirit, who creates the communal harmony. The positive side of testing the Spirit is found in the First Letter of John. The author tells his readers, "Beloved, do not believe every spirit, but test the spirits to see whether they are from God" (1 John 1:4). The "spirit that confesses that Jesus Christ has come in the flesh is from God," states the author (1 John 4:2), whereas "every spirit that does not confess Jesus is not from God" (1 John 4:3a). Thus, one knows the Spirit of God by the truth of the incarnation of the Son. Simultaneously, one also knows the spirit of error when the incarnation of the Son is not declared. The Johannine author concludes: "Whoever knows God listens to us, and whoever is not from God does not listen to us. From this we know the spirit of truth and the spirit of error" (1 John 4:6bc).

In a poem renewing hope for Israel, the HB (OT) prophet Isaiah portrays the LORD declaring, "... [T]hose who err in spirit will come to understanding, and those who grumble will accept instruction" (Isa 29:24). For the prophet, those who have left God and forsaken the path of righteousness will come to know the truth from those who teach them. Even prophets can be guilty of erring in spirit. Ezekiel records the word of the LORD: "Alas for the senseless prophets who follow their own spirit, and have seen nothing" (Ezek 13:3). In other words, there are prophets who speak out of their own imagination rather than what God shows them. The book of Proverbs expresses the same idea using the image of a scale: "All one's ways may be pure in one's own eyes, but the LORD weighs the spirit" (Prov 16:2). God tests the individual's intention; it is not what one thinks about himself or herself that matters; what matters is what God sees in one's spirit. In other words, Spirit tests spirit. God evaluates.

Journal/Meditation: Have you tested the Spirit positively or negatively or both? What was the result? Have you ever erred in spirit? Explain. When has the LORD weighed your spirit?

Prayer: Whoever knows you, O God, listens to your word, and whoever does not listen to your word, does not know you. Fill me with the Spirit of truth and keep far away from me the spirit of error. I ask this through your only-begotten Son, Jesus Christ, who lives and reigns with you forever and ever. Amen.

Spirit of Divination

Scripture: "One day, as we [, Paul and Silas,] were going to the place of prayer [in Philippi], we met a slave-girl who had a spirit of divination and brought her owners a great deal of money by fortune-telling." (Acts 16:16)

Reflection: The spirit of divination possessed by the slave-girl is translated literally as the pythian spirit. It is a reference of the serpent oracle at Delphi. This is the mythical serpent slain by Apollo; a shrine was erected at Delphi and staffed with prophetesses, who uttered words—oracles—purporting to be words of the deity. In moments of ecstatic prophecy, the slave-girl told fortunes; the costs for the exercise of her psychic powers were calculated by her owners and paid to them. Thus, her owners are considered to be religious merchants, who grow rich from the exploitation of their slave. However, the slave-girl, who follows the apostles, announces the truth, saying, "These men are slaves of the Most High God, who proclaim to you a way of salvation" (Acts 16:17). She, and the pythian spirit within her, acknowledges that the God Paul and Barnabas serve is higher than the one she serves. After this took place for several days, Paul said to the spirit, "'I order you in the name of Jesus Christ to come out of her.' And it came out that very hour" (Acts 16:18bc). This exorcising action, of course, removes her owners' source of income, and they bring Paul and Silas to the magistrates, who order them beaten with rods and then imprison them (Acts 16:19–24).

A similar story about a spirit of divination in the First Book of Samuel may be the source for the account found in the Acts. After Samuel dies, King Saul expels the mediums and the wizards from the land (1 Sam 28:3). Before preparing for battle against the Philistines, he consults the LORD about what he should do, but the LORD does not answer him (1 Sam 28:6). So, after consulting his servants, he discovers that there is a female medium at Endor (1 Sam 28:7). Saul disguises himself—because he is breaking his own law—before appearing before the woman of spirits, whom he visits at night. "Consult a spirit for me," he says to the woman, "and bring up for me the one whom I name to you" (1 Sam 28:8c). In a long story (1 Sam 28:8–25), he asks her to bring up Samuel from Sheol, the underworld, where the dead live, so he can consult him about what to do about the imminent battle with the Philistines. She, knowing that she takes her life in her own hands and seeking protection for breaking Saul's law, conjures Samuel, who rebukes Saul for disturbing him. Samuel also reminds Saul that the LORD has taken the kingdom from him and given it to David. Finally, Samuel tells Saul that he will die the next day in his battle with the Philistines, and they will defeat Israel's army. Thus, two unnamed women with a spirit of divination attempt to foretell the future or to discover the unknown which only God knows. God's will is revealed when Spirit connects to the spirits of those who worship him. God cannot be manipulated by the spirit of divination. The slave girl knows this, as do Paul and Silas, and the woman of spirits knows this (Deut 18:10), as do Samuel and Saul.

Journal/Meditation: What forms of the spirit of divination exist today? How does each of those forms attempt to foretell the future or to discover the unknown? Why can none of those do what they are purported to do?

Prayer: Most High God, through your Spirit you have revealed the way of salvation in the person of Jesus Christ, your Son. Keep far from me the spirit of divination, but send the Holy Spirit to inform my spirit of your will so that I may carry it out in the name of Jesus, who is Lord forever and ever. Amen.

Gliding Spirit

Scripture: Eliphaz the Temanite said to Job: "Now a word came stealing to me, my ear received the whisper of it. Amid thoughts from visions of the night, when deep sleep falls on mortals, dread came upon me, and trebling, which made all my bones shake. A spirit glided past my face; the hair of my flesh bristled. It stood still, but I could not discern its appearance. A form was before my eyes; there was silence, then I heard a voice: 'Can mortals be righteous before God? Can human beings be pure before their Maker?'" (Job 4:12–17)

Reflection: Eliphaz's first response to Job is based on his own experience of hearing whispers and seeing a vision of a gliding spirit during the night. Eliphaz's mention of deep sleep is echoed in the prophet Isaiah: ". . [T]he LORD has poured out upon you a spirit of deep sleep" (Isa 29:10). However, this deep sleep is not to present a vision of the night, but to close the prophets' eyes and cover the seers' heads because no one is listening to divine guidance (Isa 29:11–12). Earlier, in an oracle about Egypt, Isaiah had characterized this gliding spirit as being emptied from within the Egyptians in order to confound their plans even though they consult "the spirits of the dead and the ghosts and the familiar spirits" (Isa 19:3). The author of the First Book of Kings narrates a story about a gliding spirit (1 Kgs 22:1–44). Zedekiah, chief prophet among the four hundred court prophets of King Ahab of Israel, tells the king that he should go into battle. However, a lone prophet named Micaiah accuses the court prophets of having a lying spirit. As soon as he has spoken, Zedekiah slaps Micaiah on the cheek to show contempt and asks, "Which way did the spirit of the LORD pass from me to speak to you?" (1 Kgs 22:24; 2 Chr 18:23) In other words, Zedekiah tells Micaiah that if he and the four hundred court prophets have consulted the LORD and have the same Spirit he pretends to have, how is it possible that the same Spirit tells them one thing and tells Micaiah the contrary thing? From Zedekiah's perspective, it is impossible that four hundred prophets are wrong and one prophet is right. However, that is exactly the way it is. The spirit has glided away from the court prophets and come to rest on Micaiah.

The OT (A) prophet Baruch prays that the Lord will see that "the dead who are in Hades, whose spirit has been taken from their bodies, [are not able to] ascribe glory or justice to [him]" (Bar 2:17). When the spirit glides away from a body, it dies. Hades is the Greek word for Hebrew Sheol—the underworld, the netherworld, the bottom story of a three-story universe—the place where the dead, gliding spirits live. In a similar vein, the OT (A) book of Wisdom makes it clear that God alone has power over life and death; he can lead mortals down to the gates of Hades and back again (Wis 16:13). "A person in wickedness kills another," states the author of Wisdom, "but cannot bring back the departed spirit, or set free the imprisoned soul" (Wis 16:14). Only God has the power to give back life to a gliding spirit. The advice found in the OT (A) book of Sirach is appropriate here: "When the dead is at rest, let his remembrance rest too, and be comforted for him when his spirit has departed" (Sir 38:23). Eliphaz's questions to Job can now be answered. Mortals cannot be righteous before God unless God makes them so. Human beings cannot be pure before their Maker unless their Maker makes them so. And a gliding spirit cannot be returned to life unless the Spirit makes it so.

Journal/Meditation: Have you ever experienced a spirit gliding past you? How did it appear? What form did it take? Did it speak or was there silence?

Prayer: LORD God, when deep sleep falls on people, you may send them visions of the night. Only you have the power to bring back a departed spirit or to set free an imprisoned soul. Grant than when my spirit glides away that you will unite it deeply to your Spirit that I may ascribe glory and praise to you, Father, Son, and Holy Spirit, one God, forever and ever. Amen.

Bibliography

"Appendices." In *The Roman Missal: Study Edition*, 1415–1480. Collegeville, MN: Liturgical, 2012.

"Appendix to the Order of Mass." In *The Roman Missal: Study Edition*, 755–797. Collegeville, MN: Liturgical, 2012.

"Blessings at the End of Mass and Prayers over the People." In *The Roman Missal: Study Edition*, 674–689. Collegeville, MN: Liturgical, 2012.

Boyer, Mark G. *Divine Presence: Elements of Biblical Theophanies*. Eugene, OR: Wipf and Stock, 2017.

———. *Shhh! The Sound of Sheer Silence: A Biblical Spirituality that Transforms*. Eugene, OR: Wipf and Stock, 2019.

Catechism of the Catholic Church. Washington, DC: United States Catholic Conference, 1994.

"Common of Doctors of the Church." In *The Roman Missal: Study Edition*, 1088–90. Collegeville, MN: Liturgical, 2012.

"Common of Holy Men and Women." In *The Roman Missal: Study Edition*, 1097–1115. Collegeville, MN: Liturgical, 2012.

"Common of Martyrs." In *The Roman Missal: Study Edition*, 1052–70. Collegeville, MN: Liturgical, 2012.

"Common of Pastors." In *The Roman Missal: Study Edition*, 1017–87. Collegeville, MN: Liturgical, 2012.

"Common of the Blessed Virgin Mary." In *The Roman Missal: Study Edition*, 1039–1051. Collegeville, MN: Liturgical, 2012.

"Common of the Dedication of a Church." In *The Roman Missal: Study Edition*, 1032–1038. Collegeville, MN: Liturgical, 2012.

"Easter Sunday of the Resurrection of the Lord: The Easter Vigil in the Holy Night." In *The Roman Missal: Study Edition*, 341–86, pars. 1–70. Collegeville, MN: Liturgical, 2012.

Encarta: World English Dictionary. NY: St. Martin, 1999.

"Friday of the Passion of the Lord [Good Friday]." In *The Roman Missal: Study Edition*, 314–338. Collegeville, MN: Liturgical, 2012.

"General Instruction of the Roman Missal, The." In *The Roman Missal: Study Edition*, 17–87. Collegeville, MN: Liturgical, 2012.

Kelly, Jean P. "Word by Word." *U.S. Catholic* 84:4 (2019) 45–46.

"Masses and Prayers for Various Needs and Occasions." In *The Roman Missal: Study Edition*, 1235–1324. Collegeville, MN: Liturgical, 2012.

"Masses for the Dead." In *The Roman Missal: Study Edition*, 1369–1413. Collegeville, MN: Liturgical, 2012.

McKenzie, John. L. *Dictionary of the Bible*. Milwaukee, WI: Bruce Publishing, 1965.

New American Bible Revised Edition, The. Washington, DC: Confraternity of Christian Doctrine, 2010.

Order of Blessing the Oil of Catechumens and of the Sick and of Consecrating the Chrism, The. Washington, DC: United States Conference of Catholic Bishops, 2019.

Order of Celebrating Matrimony. Totowa, NJ: Catholic Book Publishing, 2016.

Order of Confirmation, The. Washington, DC: United States Conference of Catholic Bishops, 2016.

"Order of Mass, The." In *The Roman Missal: Study Edition*, 511–673, pars. 1–146. Collegeville, MN: Liturgical, 2012.

"Ordinary Time." In *The Roman Missal: Study Edition*, 459–494. Collegeville, MN: Liturgical, 2012.

"Ordination of a Bishop." In *The Roman Pontifical*, 217–236. Washington, DC: International Commission on English in the Liturgy, 1978.

"Ordination of a Deacon." In *The Roman Pontifical*, 173–186. Washington, DC: International Commission on English in the Liturgy, 1978.

"Ordination of a Priest." In *The Roman Pontifical*, 203–216. Washington, DC: International Commission on English in the Liturgy, 1978.

"Ordination of Bishops." In *The Roman Pontifical*, 237–254. Washington, DC: International Commission on English in the Liturgy, 1978.

"Ordination of Deacons." In *The Roman Pontifical*, 155–172. Washington, DC: International Commission on English in the Liturgy, 1978.

"Ordination of Priests." In *The Roman Pontifical*, 187–202. Washington, DC: International Commission on English in the Liturgy, 1978.

Pastoral Care of the Sick: Rites of Anointing and Viaticum. Collegeville, MN: Liturgical, 1983.

"Pentecost Sunday." In *The Roman Missal: Study Edition*, 445–457, pars. 1–13. Collegeville, MN: Liturgical, 2012.

"Proper of Saints." In *The Roman Missal: Study Edition*, 799–1027. Collegeville, MN: Liturgical, 2012.

"Proper of Time." In *The Roman Missal: Study Edition*, 137–296. Collegeville, MN: Liturgical, 2012.

Rite of Baptism for Children. Collegeville, MN: Liturgical, 1970.

Rite of Christian Initiation of Adults. Washington, DC: United States Catholic Conference, 1988.

Rite of Penance. Totowa, NJ: Catholic Book Publishing, 2009.

"Ritual Masses." In *The Roman Missal: Study Edition*, 1117–1233. Collegeville, MN: Liturgical, 2012.

Rohr, Richard. "An Interior Faith." Center for Action and Contemplation. Februry 26, 2019. http://cac.org.

———. "Coherence and Belonging." Center for Action and Contemplation. February 19, 2019. http://cac.org.

———. "Connecting to the Eternal." Center for Action and Contemplation. December 19, 2018. http://cac.org.

———. "Cosmic Notion of the Christ, A." *The Mendicant* 9:1 (2019) 1–2.

———. "From the Beginning of Time." Center for Action and Contemplation. December 3, 2018. http://cac.org.

———. "Knowing Our Source." Center for Action and Contemplation. December 10, 2018. http://cac.org.

———. "Listening as Divine Likeness." Center for Action and Contemplation. December 27, 2018. http://cac.org.

———. "Open Heart, Mind, and Body." Center for Action and Contemplation. December 9, 2018. http://cac.org.

———. "Perceiving Reality." Center for Action and Contemplation. December 18, 2018. http://cac.org.

———. "Sustaining Awareness." Center for Action and Contemplation. December 20, 2018. http://cac.org.

———. *Universal Christ, The: How a Forgotten Reality Can Change Everything We See, Hope For, and Believe*. New York: Convergent, 2019.

Roman Missal, The: Study Edition. Collegeville, MN: Liturgical, 2012.

Roman Pontifical, The. Washington, DC: International Commission on English in the Liturgy, 1978.

Scobey, Annmarie. "Keep Prayer in Mind." *U.S. Catholic* 83:5 (2018) 43–44.

Shapiro. Rami. "Roadside Assistance in the Holy Land." *Spirituality and Health* 22:1 (2019) 46–50.

Sheed, Frank. *Knowing God: God and the Human Condition*. New York: Sheed and Ward, 1966.

Thornton, David. "Lectio Intima." *Spirituality and Health* 22:2 (2019) 36–37.

"Thursday of Holy Week [Holy Thursday]: The Chrism Mass." In *The Roman Missal: Study Edition*, 290–295. Collegeville, MN: Liturgical, 2012.

"Thursday of the Lord's Supper: At the Evening Mass." In *The Roman Missal: Study Edition*, 299–313, pars. 1–44. Collegeville, MN: Liturgical, 2012.

"Votive Masses." In *The Roman Missal: Study Edition*, 1325–1366. Collegeville, MN: Liturgical, 2012.

Walsh, Carey. *Chasing Mystery: A Catholic Biblical Theology*. Collegeville, MN: Liturgical, 2012.

Recent Books by Mark G. Boyer published by Wipf & Stock

Nature Spirituality: Praying with Wind, Water, Earth, Fire

A Spirituality of Ageing

Weekday Saints: Reflections on Their Scriptures

Human Wholeness: A Spirituality of Relationship

A Simple Systematic Mariology

Praying Your Way through Luke's Gospel and the Acts of the Apostles

An Abecedarian of Animal Spirit Guides: Spiritual Growth through Reflections on Creatures

Overcome with Paschal Joy: Chanting through Lent and Easter—Daily Reflections with Familiar Hymns

Taking Leave of Your Home: Moving in the Peace of Christ

An Abecedarian of Sacred Trees: Spiritual Growth through Reflections on Woody Plants

Divine Presence: Elements of Biblical Theophanies

Fruit of the Vine: A Biblical Spirituality of Wine

Names for Jesus: Reflections for Advent and Christmas

Talk to God and Listen to the Casual Reply: Experiencing the Spirituality of John Denver

Christ Our Passover Has Been Sacrificed: A Guide through Paschal Mystery Spirituality—Mystical Theology in The Roman Missal

Rosary Primer: The Prayers, The Mysteries, and the New Testament

From Contemplation to Action: The Spiritual Process of Divine Discernment Using Elijah and Elisha as Models

All Things Mary: Honoring the Mother of God—An Anthology of Marian Reflections

Love Addict

Shhh! The Sound of Sheer Silence: A Biblical Spirituality that Transforms

www.ingramcontent.com/pod-product-compliance
Lightning Source LLC
Chambersburg PA
CBHW050812160426
43192CB00010B/1732